MW00780901

first comes
LOVE

then comes
MONEY

first comes LOVE

then comes MONEY

How Unmarried Couples Can Use Investments,
Tax Planning, Insurance, and Wills to Gain
Financial Protection Denied by Law

Larry M. Elkin

CPA and Certified Financial Planner

DOUBLEDAY CURRENCY
New York London Toronto Sydney Auckland

A Currency Book
PUBLISHED BY DOUBLEDAY
a division of Bantam Doubleday Dell Publishing Group Inc.
1540 Broadway, New York, New York 10036

Currency and Doubleday are Trademarks of Doubleday, a division of
Bantam Doubleday Dell Publishing Group, Inc.

Book Design by Gretchen Achilles

Library of Congress Cataloging-in-Publication Data

Elkin, Larry M.
    First comes love, then comes money : how unmarried
couples can use investments, tax planning, insurance and wills
to gain financial protection denied by law / Larry M. Elkin. —
1st ed.
       p.   cm.
    Includes index.
    1. Unmarried couples—United States—Finance, Personal.
2. Unmarried couples—Legal status, laws, etc.—United States.
I. Title.
HG179.E43   1994
332.024—dc20   94-9274
                                                     CIP

ISBN 0-385-47172-6
Copyright © 1994 by Larry M. Elkin
Printed in the United States of America
July 1994
First Edition

For Linda, Jessica and Alison

Acknowledgments

Most of the people who helped create this book never knew they were helping, but they deserve thanks regardless. The partners I worked for at Arthur Andersen trained me as a financial planner and freed me from corporate tax life to let me help real people solve real problems. I will always be indebted to Wallace Head, Steven Toubin, Richard Comstock, Robert Stern, Sol Upbin, and others who allowed me to launch my career in this direction. Another group of loyal, talented people at Arthur Andersen worked with me to do whatever our clients needed: Louis Rusinowitz, Marjorie Beutel, Marilyn Calister, Diane Barclay, and many others were my associates, my students, and my teachers all at once.

Stephen Rubin, Harriet Rubin, Janet Coleman, Lynn Fenwick, and the rest of the Doubleday team bought an idea and turned it into a book. My parents Rose and Harold Elkin, my brother Craig, and my in-laws Eleanor and Nicholas Field and Margaret Klein gave me a life full of affection and a conviction that everyone deserves the same. My wife Linda patiently read my drafts and guided me back to my native tongue when jargon tempted me, and our daughters Jessica and Alison spared their Daddy the evenings and weekends he needed to spend writing.

Most of all I thank the clients who have shared their lives with me, trusted me to help them make decisions, and showed me that in personal financial planning, love should always come before money.

Table of Contents

The Price of Being Different

Security, companionship, generosity, love, child rearing: These are the elements of an individual's personal happiness. Yet our laws jeopardize these privileges for unmarried domestic partners. Why do so many people, then, enter into long-term unmarried relationships? Some are homosexuals who are committed to each other but are not legally permitted to marry. Others, often elderly, share living quarters because it makes sense emotionally, medically, and financially. Still others—who may live together for as many years as traditionally married people—are philosophically and emotionally opposed to marriage.

Unmarried domestic partners are always at a disadvantage in a legal, financial, or medical emergency because as far as the law is concerned, their relationships do not exist. The only way unmarried domestic partners can take good care of each other when things go wrong is to plan carefully. This preparation entails confronting painful issues and making difficult choices. Failing to take appropriate steps can prove tragic.

Today some 3 million households are headed by couples who are not married to each other. About 1 million of these homes contain children under the age of fifteen. Heterosexuals routinely live together before marriage or without marriage, while homosexuals today are much more likely to acknowledge their preferences and their partners than they were in years past.

Being a domestic partner is financially risky. This is true whether you come from a wealthy or a modest background; whether your earning power is large or small; whether you work for yourself, your domestic partner, or someone else; whether your relationship is gay, straight, or platonic. Our laws for the most part ignore the important things that are shared in such a relationship—everything from the sofa to the money to the children. The results are often unfair and sometimes devastating.

My practice as a CPA and Certified Financial Planner has taught me, oddly enough, that money itself is not very important. Some of my wealthiest clients, and we are talking about very wealthy people indeed, are also some of the most unhappy people I know. Most of us derive satisfaction and contentment from our material success only when we can use it in the ways that meet the needs of ourselves and our loved ones. My job is to help people do that.

As I worked with a number of unmarried couples over the years, I realized how much more difficult our laws make it for them to accomplish even basic financial objectives such as supporting one another, reducing their tax burden, and providing for their children. I saw how much better my clients felt once they had confronted these issues and developed plans to overcome their legal handicaps. Because there are many more unmarried couples than I can ever hope to work with personally, I decided to write this book.

These chapters examine many aspects of living together securely and wisely. At the outset I will ask you to look at the big picture, at how the laws, customs, and business practices of our society generally treat unmarried couples. We say, in effect, to members of these relationships:

✓ **You don't exist.** One member of an unmarried couple is often treated as a legal stranger to the other. The unmarried domestic partner generally has no standing to seek custody of non–biologically related children, no right to make health-care decisions for the other, no Social Security survivor claim, no inheritance rights outside a will, no rights to a mate's pension and other employer benefits, no veteran's survivor benefits, and no standing to assume leases and other contractual rights. Also, while spouses can collect damages for the "wrongful death" of a mate, nonspouses cannot.

✓ **You don't count.** Spouses contribute to each other's welfare in many ways that are legally ignored for unmarried partners. A divorcing spouse may be entitled to alimony and will receive a portion of the couple's assets; the spouse of a retiree is entitled to a survivor's pension and Social Security benefits; a custodial parent has a right to child support from the noncustodial parent. All these things are missing in the relationship outside marriage except child support (if the noncustodial partner is a biological or adoptive parent). In some cases, the law may not recognize that one partner has an "insurable interest" in the other, which can deny important tax benefits for insurance policies.

✓ **You're just a boarder.** In the tax arena, the law generally looks at unmarried couples as roommates who perhaps happen to split expenses. Many important tax benefits available to married couples are denied. Unmarried couples cannot file a joint income tax return; this often means higher taxes. If one partner owns the home but the other pays the mortgage or property taxes, both may lose the deduction! There is also no such thing as a spousal Individual Retirement Account for a nonspouse. In the gift-tax arena, a wealthy individual who is married can give away $20,000 *per recipient* per year free of any gift tax; an unmarried individual in the same position is limited to $10,000. Also, transfers to spouses

receive an unlimited deduction for estate- and gift-tax
purposes; transfers to other domestic partners may be
fully taxable. Special estate-tax elections and basic estate-
planning techniques available to married couples are
denied to unmarried pairs.

The best defense is self-defense. This book may not make you a
financial expert, but it will alert you to the problems and offer a
range of possible solutions. In many cases you will need professional guidance to implement these suggestions. Even so, you will
get much better results if you understand the issues.

I could list many aspects of financial life in which marital status
makes a big difference, but lists can make these financial facts seem
distant and impersonal. People's lives and happiness are at stake.
Rather than make a list, let's look at some examples. These cases
are hypothetical, but they are based on real-life experiences including actual court cases.

CASE 1: Partners in Every Way

Steven and Simon were good businessmen. They became lovers and housemates when they were hired by the same architec-
tural firm just out of college. They went on to start their own firm
and began making big money when one of their clients—a hotel
developer—cut them in on a few deals. Their only real indulgence
was a lavish beach house; the rest of the money was plowed back
into the business. Then Steven died in a car accident. His share of
their wealth was $3 million. The estate tax was $1,098,000, but
Simon, the executor, did not have access to that kind of cash. He
had to sell their beach house, and some of their hotel interests as
well. He still had the architecture firm to provide him a comfortable living, but it hurt him greatly to lose the beach house with all
its memories.

The price of being different: Had Steven and Simon been married, no estate tax would have been due after Steven's death. The estate-tax law provides an unlimited "marital deduction" if the surviving spouse is a U.S. citizen. Steven and Simon wanted to formalize their relationship but no state recognizes same-sex marriages. Registering under their city's "domestic partner" ordinance did not qualify them for the estate-tax benefits.

Simon's financial grief could have been avoided if he had held an insurance policy on Steven's life. Properly arranged, such a policy would have yielded a tax-free payment to Simon. Simon could then have transferred the cash to Steven's estate (through a loan, or by buying assets) for paying the estate taxes. He would not have had to sell the beach house.

♣ CASE 2: Outliving the Breadwinner

John was a high roller. He made a fortune in the poultry business but gambled it away. John and his friends used to sit behind home plate at Yankee Stadium, betting $500 before each pitch on whether it would be a ball or a strike. In later years John mellowed a bit, taking a job at an auto-parts company that paid a decent salary plus commissions and fringes.

Carla enjoyed the ride. She didn't approve of all John's habits, but there was always enough money left over for the basics and a few luxuries. John let her save enough each month so that the children never wanted for anything. Once John retired they were able to travel to places like Florida, Europe, and Israel. Their relatives thought they were rich.

Carla and John lived together for thirty-four years without getting married. (John's parents had divorced; he bitterly referred to marriage licenses as "scrap paper.") Two years after John retired, his doctors found colon cancer, and six months later John was dead. The pension checks stopped coming.

Carla was devastated both emotionally and financially. Only fourteen states and the District of Columbia* recognize common-law marriages, and her state (New York) is not among them. Since she had never worked, she would receive no Social Security. John left no insurance. Carla was forced to move in with her daughter, but when she became ill her daughter could not care for her. After much searching they found a nursing home that had space for Carla and would accept Medicaid.

The price of being different: Carla would have been financially secure if John's pension had not stopped with his death. Since 1984, federal law has required that married individuals receive pensions that continue paying benefits to a surviving spouse, unless the spouse waives that right. Being unmarried, John was entitled to take a pension that paid only as long as he was alive—which is what he did, since this gave him the largest monthly benefit. John never even thought about what Carla would do if he died first. Had John and Carla been married she also would have been eligible for Social Security survivor benefits.

Carla could have done several things to protect herself. She could have pressed John to put away more money toward retirement; she could have insisted that he take his pension in the form of a survivor annuity that would provide for her after his death; or she could have held insurance on his life. Of course, without John's cooperation (and money) none of these steps would be possible, in which event Carla would have realized years ahead of time how precarious her own financial position had become.

---

* States recognizing common-law marriage include Alabama, Colorado, Florida, Georgia, Idaho, Iowa, Kansas, Montana, Ohio, Oklahoma, Pennsylvania, Rhode Island, South Carolina, and Texas, as well as the District of Columbia.

▲ CASE 3: The Older Lover

Victoria was shocked when Wilbur told her he needed her. Wilbur was seventy-eight, a childless widower with so much money one would think he didn't need anything. Victoria was twenty-nine and a successful model; in fact, she met Wilbur while doing a shoot for one of his companies. Victoria had recently been in a bad relationship. When Wilbur began calling, she welcomed his kindness and attention.

Next there were gifts. Money. Jewelry. Cars. An apartment. Travel, with Wilbur and on her own. She objected at first, but Wilbur insisted that he wanted to see his money make her happy.

Then Wilbur died. About eighteen months later, Victoria received a notice demanding $944,000 in back income taxes, plus interest and penalties. Her lawyers argued that Wilbur had merely been a generous friend to Victoria, and she a loving companion to him. But they faced a determined coalition in the IRS, Wilbur's executor, and the charities who were to benefit from Wilbur's estate. All these parties, who would have lost money if Victoria's argument was sustained, noted that Wilbur never filed a gift tax return. The IRS insisted that Wilbur's generosity to Victoria represented payment for sex and other "services rendered." Whether legal or not, those payments were taxable income. Victoria eventually settled by paying the government $600,000, roughly the amount she could raise by selling everything Wilbur had given her.

The price of being different: Had Wilbur married Victoria before giving her the gifts, the dispute would never have happened. (The estate would have acknowledged the gifts and claimed the marital deduction to avoid any tax due.) Even if he had married her after giving most of the gifts, she would have been better off; it would have strengthened her argument that he gave the gifts for emotional rather than commercial reasons. The government used Victoria's unmarried status against her. The IRS pointed out that Wilbur's expert advisors, and presumably Wilbur, knew that giving Victoria large gifts without marrying her would generate huge tax bills; therefore, he probably did not intend the items he gave her to be gifts.

What could Victoria have done? She could have asked Wilbur to state, preferably in writing but at least in front of witnesses, that the items he was giving her were intended to be gifts. She could have maintained a diary that recorded the items she received and Wilbur's explanation for why he was giving them to her. She could have saved letters, cards, and other documents that showed the close and affectionate relationship she enjoyed with him. And, of course, after discussing the financial as well as personal implications, Wilbur and Victoria might well have decided to get married—in which case it would have been prudent to get doctors and other witnesses to attest that Wilbur was in full possession of his faculties and not subject to undue influence by Victoria.

ⅰ CASE 4: Who Gets the Baby?

Arlene was married and divorced within three years of leaving college. She had never been able to commit to Benjamin, or to admit to herself the reasons why. Finally she met Paula and she knew; she found herself in love for the first time. Paula moved into Arlene's apartment. When they decided to raise a child Arlene became pregnant by artificial insemination. Bonnie was a gorgeous little girl, and Paula was every bit as devoted to her as Arlene was. Bonnie called her "Mommy Paula," while Arlene was simply "Mommy."

Arlene came home one Friday with a fever, which turned into raging pneumonia overnight. By the time Paula rushed her to the hospital on Saturday morning it was too late. Arlene, age twenty-nine, died Saturday evening, without leaving a will.

Paula tried to be strong for Bonnie, who was now three. She told Bonnie that Mommy was with God, but Mommy Paula would always love her and be with her. She spoke to counselors, psychiatrists, the teachers at Bonnie's preschool. Ten days after Arlene's death Bonnie seemed to be adjusting, though she clung to Paula more than usual and had regressed in her toilet training.

Then Arlene's parents sued for custody of Bonnie. They had skipped the funeral and Paula learned that they blamed her for not getting medical attention sooner for Arlene. They said Paula was irresponsible, unmarried, Lesbian, and focused on her career —a much less suitable guardian for Bonnie than Arlene's parents, Bonnie's only blood relatives, who had money, time, and a comfortable home.

Paula protested that she had always been Bonnie's parent. Each side had experts to support its case. Bonnie felt threatened, refused to talk to the judge, then had a messy accident right in his chambers. A week later, the judge awarded full custody to Arlene's parents. Paula had no visitation rights, and Arlene's parents refused to let her see Bonnie again.

The price of being different: Family-court judges have a mandate to protect the interests of young children as well as wide latitude in applying that mandate. Had Arlene left a will naming Paula as Bonnie's guardian, a judge would probably have given great weight to Arlene's wishes, although he still could have overruled it by finding Paula unfit. As it was, the judge had no guidance from Arlene and followed tradition in awarding Bonnie's custody to her nearest legal kin.

By far the best planning would have been for Arlene to leave a will naming Bonnie's guardian and a suitable alternate. Alternatively, in some states, Paula might have been allowed to adopt Bonnie legally while Arlene was alive. (In one Georgia case, such an adoption was allowed even though homosexual conduct is illegal in that state.) Homosexuals who are not the biological or adoptive parent can generally expect a difficult time convincing judges to award them custody of young children—and in many cases, heterosexuals may have almost as much difficulty.

▪ CASE 5: Tarnish on the Golden Years

Betty's husband died during the Depression, when she was a young woman, and she never remarried. A career woman ahead of her time—especially in the small midwestern city where she lived—she maintained her own apartment for several years, then took in her sister Mary and Mary's husband Sam when Sam was having trouble getting work. Childless herself, Betty helped raise Mary's children and managed the household's finances while Mary kept house and Sam worked intermittently. Betty retired in 1976. When Sam died two years later, Betty and Mary were on their own.

They were the classic odd couple, opposite in temperament and squabbling constantly, but they needed each other. Mary said she longed to die before Betty because she did not want to face life without her. But it was Betty who died first, in 1989, at the age of eighty-four.

Mary's landlord evicted her because Betty's was the only name on the lease; under the city's rent-control law the landlord could make more money renting to a new tenant. Because the household funds were in a bank account in Betty's name, the bank refused to let Mary have the money pending a probate court's ruling. Betty had not left a will. Mary had to hire a lawyer, who eventually arranged to have other family members (Betty's nieces and nephews from her late husband's side of the family) renounce their interest in her estate. But for seven months Mary had no apartment and only her Social Security check to live on; she spent most of that time shuttling between children in Houston and Chicago. Once the bank account was released, Mary was able to return to her city and rent a furnished room, but her financial troubles and her loneliness left her depressed and in failing health. Scarcely a year after Betty's death, Mary suffered a fatal stroke.

The price of being different: Most Americans, married or otherwise, have no will. Their assets are disposed of in two ways. Certain assets, called *probate assets,* are transferred according to their state's laws on *intestacy* (someone dying without a will is said to be "intestate"). Other assets, most notably those held as joint tenants with right of survivorship, go to the surviving owners automatically ("by operation of law," in technical terms). The intestacy laws generally give spouses and surviving children priority in claiming the deceased's assets. No special treatment is given to a particular relative merely for having lived with the deceased.

A few simple steps could have made Mary's life much easier. The household bank account should have been held as joint tenants with right of survivorship, rather than solely in Betty's name; this would have avoided any freezing of assets. Likewise, had Mary cosigned the lease, she likely would have kept her apartment. (Local laws can have a big impact on this. In some cities, even cohabiting individuals who have not signed the lease retain rights to an apartment; in other places, the presence of unmarried people in a household may violate zoning rules in single-family neighborhoods.) Finally, Betty could have left a will giving her possessions to Mary; this would have greatly simplified the probate process.

Domestic partners face a broad range of financial-planning problems. The good news is that most of them can be solved, or at least properly addressed. In the course of this book I will show how to do just that.

2

Sharing Lives

Many couples choose to remain unmarried, while others (notably homosexuals) cannot legally marry. Within both of these groups, the degree of sharing and mutual commitment varies enormously. Certainly, this is true of married couples as well: While some couples share everything (both emotionally and legally), others divide their property into baskets called *Yours, Mine,* and *Ours.*

Financial planning for unmarried couples begins with a basic issue: Is this plan for Me or for Us? Usually, the answer will include elements of both, but the mixture will vary almost infinitely. You cannot have a successful financial plan unless you understand your objectives. Thus, if personal finance is on your mind, you have to make your goals clear to yourself and to your domestic partner as well.

In my experience, there are five types of domestic-partner relationships. Of course these are generalizations, and a particular couple may progress through various types of relationships (in either direction) over time. Still, to find a starting point for your planning, find where you fit in this scheme:

The Roommates. You are cohabiting for convenience, either financial or personal. The relationship is likely to be temporary.

Often, though not always, it is platonic; one or both partners may have one or more romantic interests outside the relationship. Most often, people in these relationships will either be rather young (college students or not far removed) or rather old (often finding a roommate after losing a mate). Their financial lives are as separate as possible; to the extent they plan for each other, the planning is often defensive (such as how to avoid being responsible for debts incurred by the other).

The Test Drivers. You know you want to be together now; the future is still cloudy. You may be a couple that has dated for some time and now wants to be together more, a two-career couple whose best chance of finding time together is at home, or a couple whose go-slow philosophy is a result of past unsuccessful relationships. Sometimes, especially with younger people, living together is a way of setting up house while other elements of life (such as the type and location of post-graduation jobs) are still undetermined. Test drivers generally keep their financial lives separate, although they do not mind joining forces on relatively small or short-term investments (home electronics, or perhaps even a car). They may maintain a small joint account for household expenses, since having "your" tuna fish and "my" mayonnaise is both picayune and unromantic.

The Newly (Un)Weds. Make no mistake about it—you are in love. Living together is the only way you can get enough of each other (and even that may not suffice). If of opposite gender, you already may be thinking of marriage, but any wedding plans are far into the future. Why? Maybe because the relationship is so new, albeit intense, that one or both of you have doubts about how gracefully it will age. Or maybe education plans, military obligations, or similar commitments make an early wedding impractical. For now, things are great. You are definitely more committed to each other than the Test Drivers, but you still have not said "I do." On the financial front, joint commitments such as bank accounts, a car, and even liquid investments seem reasonable. But buying a house or financing the partner's education may provoke a gulp and some hesitation; these investments can be difficult to divide or recoup if something goes wrong.

The Committed Couple. You may not have uttered the words " 'Til death do us part," but that spirit is in your heart. Of course there is always a chance things will not work out (after all, nearly half of legal first marriages end in divorce); however, the promise has been sincerely made. There are many reasons why a legal marriage may not take place: homosexuality, reluctance to terminate the alimony rights of one partner, religious or social impediments to divorce from a prior relationship. For you, the planning objective often will be to duplicate, as far as possible, the rights and protection that the law affords a married couple. Being the most deeply involved in an alternative lifestyle, the Committed Couple clearly is exposed to the greatest financial risks.

The Open Couple. This type of relationship is probably very rare regardless of age or sexual orientation. It involves two people who intend to remain together indefinitely, but who either tolerate or expect that their partner will have close personal relationships with others. The staying power of this kind of arrangement seems very questionable, though perhaps not to the individuals involved. This type of couple may be prepared to make substantial long-term commitments and would perhaps deny that they are at all different from the Committed Couple. Perhaps, but as a financial planner, I would probably try to supply choices that are as flexible as possible in case the relationship changes or ends.

Of course it will happen occasionally that each member of a couple will place himself or herself in different categories, which is unpleasant for those involved. The problem is the dissimilar expectations each member has for the relationship, not with the financial-planning process that brings those differences to the surface. Financially and personally, the pain is usually minimized by identifying and addressing these problems early.

Should you share your financial planning with your partner? Probably yes, if you are part of a Committed Couple (although even many married couples are not completely involved in each other's finances). In other categories, the sharing is going to be limited to varying degrees. Each couple will have to strike its own balance.

Going On the Record

You cannot share information that you don't have. Unfortunately, for most of us, our own financial situation looks like a medieval map of the world. The ground around us is pretty well understood, but the more remote points are likely to be *terra incognita*. Financial planning begins at the beginning—by understanding where you are today.

The basic elements of a financial plan include the following:

✓ personal data identifying your age, Social Security number, citizenship, state of domicile, marital status, and close relatives

✓ a listing of key advisors, bank and brokerage houses, safe-deposit boxes, and other information to assist in locating your assets and verifying your debts

✓ a Net Worth Statement that lists, in the form of a financial statement or balance sheet, your assets and your debts, including potential tax liability if assets were to be sold

✓ a budget that lists anticipated income and expenses for the next twelve months.

Personal Data—The Key Facts List

A Key Facts List is reproduced here for immediate reference and in the Appendix at the end of this book for easy photocopying. This list is designed to produce a "paper trail" that can help you, or your advisors or heirs, locate the people and documents that control your financial life. You should leave the copy in the back of the book blank and use photocopies to make your entries. This will make it easier for you to update the list in the future. You should update it once a year or whenever you engage in a significant transaction (such as buying a large insurance policy). Alternatively, you might want to enter this data into a computer and update it there— but if you do, remember to keep backup copies!

The Key Facts List is a very important document; it can help ensure that your heirs do not overlook any of your assets or pay debts that perhaps you did not owe. You should give it to your attorney, your domestic partner, or another trusted individual to keep together with your will and other vital papers. *Do not* place it in a safe-deposit box under your own name. If you die, the box may be sealed for a time while probate takes place, and the list must be available during probate if it is to do much good. (Probate is the court process that disposes of your assets according to your state's inheritance laws.)

Key Facts List

Name:

Date Prepared:

Personal Data:

Birth Date: _____

Social Security Number: _____

Location of Principal Home: _____

Location of Other Homes: _____

Citizen of: _____

Domestic Partner

Name: _____

Birth Date: _____

Social Security Number: _____

Location of Principal Home: _____

Location of Other Homes: _____

Citizen of: _____

Child #1

Name: _____

Birth Date: _____

Social Security Number: _____

Custodial Parent: _____

Address & Phone: _____

Is Child Married ? (Y/N): _____

Spouse's Name: _____

Location of Principal Home: _____

Location of Other Homes: _____

Citizen of: _____

Child's Dependents: _____

_____

_____

Child #2

Name: _____

Birth Date: _____

Social Security Number: _____

Custodial Parent: _____

Address & Phone: _____

Is Child Married ? (Y/N): _____

Spouse's Name: _____

Location of Principal Home: _____

Location of Other Homes: _____

Citizen of: _____

Child's Dependents: _____

_____

_____

Child #3

Name: _____

Birth Date: _____

Social Security Number: _____

Custodial Parent: _____

Address & Phone: _____

Is Child Married ? (Y/N): _____

Spouse's Name: _____

Location of Principal Home: _____

Location of Other Homes: _____

Citizen of: _____

Child's Dependents: _____

_____

_____

Key Facts List

Financial Advisors

Attorney (business):
Firm Name: _____
Street Address: _____
City, State, ZIP: _____
Telephone: _____

Attorney (personal):
Firm Name: _____
Street Address: _____
City, State, ZIP: _____
Telephone: _____

Accountant (business):
Firm Name: _____
Street Address: _____
City, State, ZIP: _____
Telephone: _____

Accountant (personal):
Firm Name: _____
Street Address: _____
City, State, ZIP: _____
Telephone: _____

Life Insurance Agent:
Company: _____
Street Address: _____
City, State, ZIP: _____
Telephone: _____

Employer:
Firm Name: _____
Street Address: _____
City, State, ZIP: _____
Telephone: _____

Property/Casualty Agent:
Company: _____
Street Address: _____
City, State, ZIP: _____
Telephone: _____

Stockbroker:
Firm Name: _____
Street Address: _____
City, State, ZIP: _____
Telephone: _____

Financial Planner:
Firm Name: _____
Street Address: _____
City, State, ZIP: _____
Telephone: _____

Banker (business):
Firm Name: _____
Street Address: _____
City, State, ZIP: _____
Telephone: _____

Banker (personal):
Firm Name: _____
Street Address: _____
City, State, ZIP: _____
Telephone: _____

Physician:
Firm/Hospital: _____
Street Address: _____
City, State, ZIP: _____
Telephone: _____

Key Facts List

Document Locator

Document	Doc. Date	Location	Notes
Contracts			
Marital/Premarital/Living			
Business Buy/Sell			
Employment			
Partnership			
Other			
Property Records			
Bank Statements			
Brokerage Statements			
Employee Benefit Statements			
Stock Certificates			
Bonds, Promissory Notes			
Automobile Title			
Boat Title			
Other Personal Property Title			
Personal Property Inventory			
Primary Residence Closing Papers			
Vacation Home Closing Papers			
Other Real Estate Closing Papers			
Cemetery Plot Title			
List of Real Estate Improvements			
Mortgages			
Personal Records			
Birth Certificate			
Baptismal Records			
Divorce Papers			
Marriage License			
Medical Records			
Passport			
Immigration/Naturalization Papers			
Social Security Card			
Income Tax Returns			
Gift Tax Returns			
Tax Records			
Income Tax Returns			
Gift Tax Returns			
Receipts, Cancelled Checks, etc.			
Insurance Records			
Life Insurance Policies			
Health Insurance Policies			
Disability Insurance Policies			
Homeowner's Policies			
Other Policies			
Estate Planning			
Will			
Trust Agreements			
Living Will			
Durable Power of Attorney			
Health-Care Power of Attorney			
Funeral Instructions			

The Net Worth Statement

If you have any accounting training you will probably recognize that the Net Worth Statement is just a balance sheet that has been adapted to the needs of an individual rather than a business. The formula for determining net worth is simple:

What you have – What you owe = Your net worth

The Net Worth Statement does far more, however, than just tell you how rich you are. It can provide considerable insight into your financial position. Let's compare the Net Worth Statements of Richard and Susan, each of whom have net worth of $250,000:

	RICHARD		**SUSAN**
Assets		**Assets**	
Cash	$ 1,000	Cash	$ 25,000
Stocks & Bonds	10,000	Stocks & Bonds	100,000
IRAs	39,000	IRAs	0
House	$400,000	House	$125,000
Total Assets	$450,000	Total Assets	$250,000
Debts		**Debts**	
Student Loan	$ 10,000		0
Mortgage	190,000		
Total Debts	$200,000		
Net Worth	$250,000	Net Worth	$250,000

The differences are obvious. Richard has sizable debts and very little cash with which to pay them; his wealth is tied up in his home and in retirement accounts which he can tap only by paying taxes and perhaps penalties. Susan, on the other hand, has a comfortable cash reserve, no debt, owns her home free and clear, and has a well-balanced stock-and-bond portfolio that probably provides her with both income and capital growth. So while they have the same net worth, their financial positions are distinctly different.

Do not jump to the conclusion that Susan's financial position is *better* than Richard's. All we know at this point is that it is *different.* Perhaps Susan has significant family obligations or is very conservative while Richard is unattached and inclined to take risks with his money. Perhaps Richard is expecting a very large salary or bonus this year. Richard may also be saving for retirement in a manner that has considerable tax advantages, while Susan is not. As long as Richard can understand and accept the financial hazards he faces, his portfolio may be perfectly appropriate for him. Later in this book we will describe how to build the financial structure that is appropriate for you.

The Net Worth Statement lists everything you have and everyone you owe, and you will want to keep this very personal information confidential. But you *must* share this information with the following:

✓ your estate planners (attorney, accountant, or both)

✓ your stockbroker, insurance agent, and other investment advisors

✓ your banker, if the information is relevant to some credit need (for example, in applying for a large mortgage or a business loan)

✓ your executor (by leaving a copy of the Net Worth Statement together with your will and the Key Facts List).

You don't have to give your domestic partner this information, at least while you are alive. Of course, you may *want* your partner to have this information. Generally, the more committed and long-term the relationship, the more important it is to share this type of data (since various income- and estate-tax strategies may be possible if you and your partner are willing to collaborate). If you are part of a Committed Couple, make certain your attorneys, accountants, and other advisors are aware of this commitment since they cannot properly advise you otherwise.

The Budget

Most people intuitively understand the value of a written household budget. Yet few people ever actually establish a budget, and even fewer use one correctly by carefully monitoring actual expenses and comparing them to the budget plan.

As a result, many people have only a vague idea of where their money goes. Financial planners call this *the evaporative effect of money*. A budget is the lid you place over your pot of money to keep it from evaporating.

Your budget has to accommodate five different uses for your cash:

✓ **Fixed expenses**—items like rent, mortgage payments, other debt service, commuting, car payments, etc., over which you have relatively little month-to-month control. (This is not to say you have *no* control. In fact, probably the greatest single source of financial distress is an unwise decision to increase fixed costs, such as buying a too-expensive home. You don't set fixed-cost levels often, but when you do it has a major impact on your finances.)

✓ **Variable expenses**—items over which you have more control in the short term. Clothing, recreation,

Net Worth Statement

Name: **Assets:**   **Date:**

	Current Value	Tax Cost (A)	Potential Tax on Sale (B)	Net Value
Liquid				
Cash (checking, savings accounts)				
Short-term investments				
Treasury bills				
Savings certificates				
Money market funds				
Cash value of life insurance				
Total Liquid Assets				
Investment				
Notes receivable				
Publicly traded stocks				
Taxable bonds				
Tax-exempt bonds				
Investment real estate				
Non-marketable securities				
Retirement funds				
Other				
Total Investment Assets				
Personal				
Principal residence				
Vacation property				
Art, antiques				
Furnishings				
Vehicles				
Boats				
Other				
Total Personal Assets				
Total Assets				

NOTES:

(A): Tax cost, or basis, is the amount you are deemed to have invested in the asset for tax purposes. The greater the basis, the less the potential tax if you decide to sell the asset.

(B): Potential tax on sale is the estimated tax you would pay if you sold the asset. You compute this by subtracting the tax cost from the market value of the asset, then multiplying by the tax rate. (For many taxpayers, asset sales are likely to be taxed at more favorable capital gains rates.) Your true net worth is the market value of your assets less this accrued tax. Note that under present law, however no capital gains tax would be due on assets you bequeath to others when you die, because the assets receive a new tax basis equal to the fair market value of your death (a "stepped-up basis").

Net Worth Statement

Liabilities

	Current Value	Net Value
Short Term (Due in Less Than 2 Years)		
Credit Card debt	_____	_____
Auto, boat, etc. loans	_____	_____
Installment loans	_____	_____
Education loans	_____	_____
Borrowings on life insurance	_____	_____
Brokerage margin accounts	_____	_____
Other debt	_____	_____
Total Short-Term Liabilities	_____	_____
Long Term (Due in More Than 2 Years)		
Loans to purchase personal assets	_____	_____
Loan to acquire business	_____	_____
Mortgages	_____	_____
Total Long-Term Liabilities	_____	_____
Total Liabilities	_____	_____
Total Net Worth	_____	_____

entertainment, and luxury items and services are in this category. When people try to cut their budget, they usually start here. Unfortunately, these expenses account for a relatively small share of spending and, often, the budget cut just defers this spending rather than eliminating it.

✓ **Short-term savings and investment**—savings for needs that are expected within a year or two. A down payment on a home, a car, or a return to school are often major items in this category.

✓ **Medium-term savings and investment**—savings for needs that are expected within a range of about two to ten years. Children's education, retirement, and starting a business can be big items in this area.

✓ **Long-term savings and investment**—retirement and children's education start out in this category, which represents savings for needs not expected to arise for at least ten years, and then move to medium- and short-term categories as those events draw closer. Wealthy families often establish trusts to benefit children, grandchildren, and other heirs, some of whom may not even be born yet; providing for these future generations also is a form of long-term investment.

The budget categories listed above form a hierarchy. Fixed expenses tend to crowd out variable expenses, which bump against short-term savings, which cut into medium-term investment, which displaces long-term savings. *Financial planning is the art of striking a rational balance among these competing needs.*

Your domestic partner has a significant impact on your budget no matter what the nature of your relationship. It is nearly impossible to cut fixed expenses significantly without affecting your partner, so cooperation can be critical. Variable expenses, also, may be difficult to control without your partner's participation—if all meals are eaten in restaurants because your partner cannot or will not help in the kitchen, you will probably have trouble controlling costs.

Fortunately, most people are more willing to share budget information, both income and expense, than they would be to share information on their net worth. The majority of couples probably have a good idea of their mate's income, and perhaps spending as well. Even Roommates routinely share this information.

A household budget, then, is a joint enterprise, although in setting that budget you may have to reconcile differing financial needs of each partner. (Don't be surprised, however, if some conflict arises in the course of developing a joint budget. I have witnessed more than one heated argument erupt in my office between members of a couple as we went over their spending plans.)

The budget provides a starting point. It is a good idea to go back through your check register and credit-card records for the past year to get a reasonably accurate sense of how you spend your money. Don't waste time being overly precise in the categories; for practical purposes, entertainment spending is the same regardless of whether you are paying for parking, theater tickets, or restaurants.

Setting Goals

Your Net Worth Statement tells you what you have already accumulated; your budget tells you how you are using the funds that come in. Now you need to set financial goals so that you can make appropriate changes.

The goal-setting process is the core of financial planning. Committed Couples, Open Couples, and perhaps Newly (Un)Weds usually will need to agree on these goals or risk serious friction. Roommates and Test Drivers will probably start by setting their own individual goals and merging them later if the relationship proves to be lasting.

Household Budget

Income	Current Year	Next Year (est.)
Your Salary		
Your Bonus		
Domestic Partner Salary (Opt.)		
Domestic Partner Bonus (Opt.)		
Other Compensation		
Dividends		
Interest		
Capital Gains		
Other		
Other		
Total Income		

Expenses	Current Year	Next Year (est.)
Fixed Expenses		
Taxes & Withholding		
Groceries		
Mortgage		
Other Loans & Credit Cards		
Property Tax		
Utilities		
Home Maintenance		
Clothing & Dry Cleaning		
Uninsured Medical & Dental		
Child Care		
Car Loans		
Gasoline & Oil		
Car Repairs & Maintenance		
Insurance: Life, Home, Car		
Tuition		
Total Fixed Expenses		
Variable Expenses		
Major Purchases		
Restaurants		
Entertainment		
Telephone		
Vacation		
Books, CDs, Magazines		
Fitness		
Personal Grooming		
Gifts		
Charitable Donations		
Other		
Total Variable Expenses		
Total Expenses		
SURPLUS OR SHORT FALL		

Many financial planners ask clients to rank specific goals, such as:

✓ maintaining or increasing current spending

✓ saving for education (their own or their children's)

✓ providing a certain level of income for retirement

✓ being able to retire at a particular age

✓ protecting survivors in case of premature death

✓ maintaining income in case of disability

✓ acquiring funds for specific needs (vacation home, new business, etc.).

Once these goals are ranked, the financial planner will make (or will ask the client to make) certain assumptions about future inflation, income, and tax rates, and will then try to rearrange the budget and investments to satisfy as many of the goals as possible. The actual mechanics of this process are too detailed to go into here, but you can either seek professional guidance or attempt to do this yourself. (It is possible to do a rough financial plan with just a calculator and a lot of paper, but computer software has come on the market in recent years to make this much easier. You might want to try *WealthBuilder by Money Magazine* for IBM-compatible PCs.)

Sharing the Wealth

From the day you moved in together you have been accumulating material possessions—maybe big items like cars, boats, and homes; maybe smaller belongings like portable CD players. Perhaps there are even intangibles such as life insurance policies and stock portfolios. Who pays for all these assets, and who owns them?

The common law governing unmarried couples in all U.S. states generally holds that the person who pays for something is the person who owns it, except when otherwise stated on a deed, title certificate, or similar document. If one of you plays the role of primary earner while the other is a struggling artist, a manager of a bookstore, or a homemaker, it is likely that the division of property will be very unequal if you break up. If this is what you intend, fine. If it isn't, you ought to do something about it.

Start by reaching an understanding with your domestic partner. If, for instance, you are a gay couple, it is not unreasonable to agree as soon as you become a Committed Couple that you intend to arrange your affairs as though you were married, to the extent this is possible. If you agree on this, an attorney might then draw up an agreement or contract which states that all property acquired while you reside together, other than that which either of you receive as a gift or inheritance, is to be owned jointly. Any income derived from such property would also be held jointly. Further, this agreement could state that should you break up the property is to be sold and the proceeds are to be split, unless you both agree otherwise at that time.

These steps do not get you to the same place exactly as a legal marriage, but they are a decent start. There is still the big problem of how the tax laws will regard your arrangement. If, for example, your agreement states that the nonbreadwinner partner is being compensated for housekeeping, companionship, and other services, this individual may owe income tax on any property he or she receives from the breadwinner. The breadwinner may even be responsible for paying Social Security and other payroll taxes for his (or her) mate! On the other hand, if the agreement is merely a statement of the breadwinner's intent to make gifts to his beloved, there are potential gift-tax consequences as well as a strong risk that a court would decline to enforce the agreement. The IRS might even view the value of housing, food, and other support provided by the breadwinner to the other partner to be taxable gifts, since the breadwinner's provision of these items is due to generosity rather than any legal obligation of support. Gift tax is only a serious concern to individuals or couples with significant assets (generally more than $600,000), as we will see in Chapter Eleven. Because of the limited application of gift tax, I would expect most unmarried couples to use the gift approach and avoid characterizing the wealth sharing as payment for services.

Another approach is what I call the Balance Sheet Method. Every year, you determine your net worth, as discussed earlier in this chapter. You compare the figure to what you calculated the previous year. At that point, the breadwinner (whose net worth probably reflects most of the increase) can make an outright gift of cash, property, or anything else to the other partner. Of course, nothing legally obliges the breadwinner to make such a gift, but if no gift is forthcoming, at least the other partner has only invested one year in the relationship without receiving what he may feel is his due. As long as both partners are moved by the spirit of fairness and equity, the ritual can become automatic and perhaps even fun, somewhat like exchanging gifts for the holidays. This kind of arrangement sounds crass, but remember that what you are doing is putting yourselves in the same position that married couples are in automatically.

The following worksheet, which is also reproduced in the Appendix, can help you implement the Balance Sheet Method in sharing your wealth.

Gifts to Domestic Partner (Balance Sheet Method)

Date:

NOTE: Some unmarried couples may want to share in the overall increase in wealth that they accumulate during their relationship, as married couples do under the law. This work-sheet allows you and your domestic partner to devise a program of annual gifts that measure and then equalize the change in your financial position. You can, of course, modify this program any way you wish, such as by removing a partner's business assets from the calculation.

	Beginning of Year			End of Year		
Assets	Partner #1	Partner #2	Total Value	Partner #1	Partner #2	Total Value
Liquid Assets	___	___	___	___	___	___
Investment Assets	___	___	___	___	___	___
Personal Assets	___	___	___	___	___	___
Total Assets	___	___	___	___	___	___
Liabilities						
Short-Term Debt	___	___	___	___	___	___
Long-Term Debt	___	___	___	___	___	___
Total Liabilities	___	___	___	___	___	___
Total Net Worth	___	___	___	___	___	___

	Partner #1	Partner #2	Difference
NET WORTH—END OF YEAR	___	___	
NET WORTH—BEGINNING OF YEAR	___	___	
INCREASE (DECREASE)	___	___	
COMPENSATING GIFT	___	50% of Difference	
(from partner with greater increase)	___	___	

Building a Partnership

A successful long-term relationship is a partnership in every way, including finances. The issues covered in this chapter can be addressed independently or together. The more long-lived the relationship, the more important it is at least to develop a common ground in financial goals and strategies so that both partners move in the same direction.

3

Estate Planning

Today you are healthy, independent, self-sufficient, able to manage your own affairs. You have your own vision of how those affairs should be organized. Developing an estate plan simply means extending that vision so that you understand, and convey to others, how your affairs are to be run when you are not able to handle them yourself.

Where There's a Will

Although you and I are strangers, I know this much about you: If you are responsible for someone else's well-being and you have not executed a will, you have a serious problem.

Wills are not just for people who have money (although anyone with money should have one). Wills are not just for people who have children (although anyone with children should *definitely* have one). Wills are for everyone who is past the recently-graduated-with-no-responsibilities stage of life.

Yet only about one quarter of adults who die do so with a valid personal will. Everybody else gets a one-size-fits-all will that has been written by their state government. Knowing that many people will shirk their responsibilities to draft a will, lawmakers have tried to create a set of assumptions that meet most of the needs of most of these people, most of the time.

Well-intentioned as they are, do these lawmakers consider the needs of unmarried domestic partners? Definitely not! These state-drafted wills, known as *intestacy laws,* are a disaster for unmarried couples. Let's look at a hypothetical case.

⚫ CASE 1: Get Thee Out

Bill was a successful investment banker whose marriage foundered amid the deals and pressures of the 1980s. His ex-wife won custody of their two young sons. Shortly after the divorce Bill met Carol, a twenty-four-year-old art student. They lived together for seven years. Bill supported Carol, whose income from teaching and painting was too small to pay for the Manhattan studio where she worked and the lovely co-op apartment where they lived. Bill, age forty-two, suffered a fatal heart attack on New Year's Eve in 1992. At his death he owned the co-op and $4 million in investments, but he had no will.

Under New York law, all of Bill's assets went to his children because he was unmarried. The court appointed Bill's ex-wife as trustee of the children's funds. Within a month, she ordered Carol to vacate the co-op so that it could be sold and the funds reinvested on behalf of the boys.

Carol fought but to no avail. The court rejected Carol's contention that Bill had implicitly agreed to support and provide for her as long as they stayed together. Carol lost her home and, soon, was forced to move her studio to much smaller quarters as well.

The big problem, of course, was Bill's failure to provide for Carol in a will. Carol was not completely helpless, however. If she were aware of Bill's failure to execute a will, she could have obtained (or asked him to obtain) an insurance policy on his life naming her as beneficiary.

There is an ironic postscript to this situation. Under New York law, if Bill's young children were to die without leaving a will, their mother (Bill's ex-wife) would inherit the estate they had received from Bill. Without a doubt this is the last thing Bill would have wanted, but that is what can happen when you let the state draft a will for you.

Nobody can make estate planning less frightening or emotional. In this chapter we will face some of the most difficult decisions you may ever have to make. Try to think of it this way: A well-written will is your way of cleaning up the mess you would otherwise leave behind. If you don't tidy up your own affairs, you put the burden on the courts, the lawyers, and most of all on your family. Carefully planning your estate is a loving and thoughtful act that takes just a little time and can spare much pain.

Estate planning deals with many issues, some of them financial, some not. These include:

✓ distributing your assets

✓ managing and settling your affairs

✓ raising your children

✓ investing and managing the assets that you leave behind for the benefit of children and other loved ones.

Drafting a will is, of course, a vital part of good estate planning, but there are several other documents that may be needed. These include:

✓ **Trusts.** A trust is a very valuable and flexible legal arrangement that has many uses in estate planning. Trusts will, therefore, be discussed frequently throughout this book, and receive a close look in Chapter Twelve.

✓ **A durable power of attorney.** This document allows someone to make decisions and take action on your behalf if you are incapacitated.

✓ **A health-care power of attorney.** This legal arrangement gives someone the authority to make medical decisions on your behalf if you are incapable of doing so.

✓ **A living will.** This document expresses your desires concerning certain types of treatment when you are terminally ill and unable to speak for yourself.

A few years ago I was introduced to a very wealthy man of seventy-three who took great pride in his carefully drawn will. The man, who we'll call Herbert, mentioned that he was divorced from his first wife, and that his son by that marriage, age thirty-seven, did not get along well with his second wife. I asked Herbert what would happen to his assets if he were to suffer a stroke or other disabling illness. He stared back at me with a worried look. I volunteered that his son and his second wife would probably end up in court fighting each other for control of the money. Herbert wasted no time in signing a durable power of attorney to ensure that control would go to his son.

On another occasion I was asked to review the estate plan of a married couple. I found that it created about $150,000 in unnecessary tax exposure, and called the husband to suggest that his wife have her will updated. That was impossible, he told me; she was in a coma with terminal cancer and was not expected to live. He did, however, hold a durable power of attorney she had executed. That same evening a friendly attorney drew up a new trust and, using the durable power, the next day the husband made gifts of some of his wife's assets to solve the estate-tax problem. The woman died ten days later.

A good estate plan places decision-making power in the hands of people we trust so that they can deal with life's contingencies for us when the need arises. Because no one knows when that will be, the time for estate planning is today.

How Assets Are Transferred at Death

For most people, the primary reason to have a will is to control how one's assets are distributed at one's death. To do a good job of planning for this eventuality, you have to understand the general rules of how property can be owned and transferred. Otherwise, you stand a good chance of creating an estate plan that does not do what you intend, and can in fact do the opposite.

We can begin by revisiting the term *probate,* which seems to intimidate a lot of people. (That's why there is a big market for books on how to avoid probate.) Probate is simply a legal process that takes the property of someone who is dead and distributes it to someone who is alive. A will, if one is executed, governs the disposition of the *probate estate,* which is the property that is disposed of through court-supervised probate proceedings. Certain other property is automatically transferred ("by operation of law") without having to go through probate proceedings.

Let's look first at property that is transferred by operation of law. This includes:

✓ **Property owned jointly (''joint tenancy'') with right of survivorship.** Ownership passes to the surviving owner(s). Except in community property states, joint ownership is the form most often used by married couples; the surviving spouse is therefore the sole owner of the property as soon as the first spouse dies. A few states (including, at this writing, Alaska, North Carolina, Pennsylvania, Tennessee, and Texas) have placed restrictions on the use of joint tenancy.

✓ **''Tenancy by the entirety.''** This arrangement is restricted to married couples. Property owned as tenants by the entirety is treated much the same way as joint tenancies, with the survivor automatically becoming the sole owner. However, unlike most joint tenancy arrangements, both parties must agree to any change in the form of ownership. About half the states and the District of Columbia recognize some form of tenancy by the entirety, but again, this arrangement only applies to married couples.

✓ **Pay-on-death accounts.** An account with a pay-on-death provision is owned by a single individual, but is automatically paid to another individual upon the owner's death. This arrangement is most often used for bank deposits.

✓ **Insurance, annuities, and other contracts.** Death benefits and other prerogatives of ownership pass to the beneficiary named in the contract (if any). If no beneficiary is named, the ownership passes to the estate of the deceased and becomes part of the probate estate.

✓ **Retirement plans, Individual Retirement Accounts, other employee benefits.** Rights to these benefits pass to the specified beneficiaries, if any. Federal law gives surviving spouses an automatic right to certain retirement benefits unless the spouse signs a waiver of those rights. However, if the deceased is unmarried and fails to name a beneficiary, benefits usually flow to his estate and become probate property.

✓ **Partnership interests.** Disposed of as provided in the partnership agreement.

✓ **Trusts.** Disposed of as provided in the deed of trust (the "trust instrument").

The use of these types of arrangements can have a tremendous impact on an unmarried couple, especially in the absence of a will. Consider the following situation:

▎ CASE 2: Who Gets the House?

Vicki was only sixteen when her son Tom was born. She worked nights as a barmaid to put herself through school and eventually became a veterinarian. She went into practice with Allen, a classmate she had been dating, and they decided to move in together. They bought a rambling old home in the country that had a carriage house suitable for an office, and plenty of space for kennels. A year later, when Tom was ten, Vicki died in a car crash. She left a will naming her mother as Tom's guardian and leaving her property to her son. However, since Vicki's money was tied up in the real estate she owned jointly with Allen, the probate estate was virtually empty, and Tom received nothing under the will.

What happened to the house? Since the property was jointly owned with Allen, he became the sole owner—in effect, becoming Vicki's sole heir. A complex legal fight ensued, as Vicki's mother sued Allen on Tom's behalf seeking a share of the property. Although they eventually settled, legal fees were high and Allen was hard pressed to scrape together some cash for the settlement. The problems could have been avoided if Vicki and Allen had owned the property as tenants in common, which would have included Vicki's share of the house in her probate estate, rather than as joint tenants.

A good estate plan will carefully coordinate the passage of non-probate property with the probate estate to ensure that the total amounts your heirs receive are consistent with your goals.

Community Property versus "Common Law"

There are special rules that govern the treatment of property acquired by married couples. These rules can be of interest to unmarried couples as well for at least three reasons. First, if either partner has been married, the application of these rules in a divorce or probate proceeding may have lasting consequences. Second, heterosexual couples usually have the option to get married, so you ought to know what the property consequences would be. Finally, couples that cannot or choose not to marry may still want to keep financial relations on par with married couples; to do this, you need to know how marital finances work so that you can duplicate them as much as possible outside marriage.

Nine states have adopted *community property* rules that govern ownership of most property acquired during the marriage. These states are Arizona, California, Idaho, Louisiana, Nevada, New Mexico, Texas, Washington, and Wisconsin. In these states, most of the wealth that is accumulated during a marriage belongs one half to each spouse regardless of whose earnings generated the wealth. It does not matter whether you were married in the community-property state; community-property status applies to assets accumulated while you live in the jurisdiction and continues to govern those assets if you later move to a non–community-property state. Of course, community-property rules only apply to legally married couples, which excludes all homosexual pairs and anybody else who has not been legally married.

Community property is probate property: Each owner can leave his or her share by will to anyone he/she chooses. This power is in sharp contrast to joint tenancy, the most common form of marital property ownership outside the community-property states, in which the surviving joint tenant automatically becomes the sole owner.

Property ownership for unmarried individuals in all fifty states, and for married individuals in the forty-one non–community-property states and the District of Columbia, is determined under *common-law* rules. These rules basically provide that an individual owns any property purchased with his or her own assets or out of his or her own income, as well as any assets in which sole ownership is shown on a title, deed, or similar legal document. Under these rules, in an unmarried couple where only one partner has assets and income, in the event of death or separation the "breadwinner" will own everything that has not been formally given to the other partner. Except in the highly unusual "palimony" cases, in which unmarried individuals have been able to win judgments against their partners, there is no such thing as "equitable distribution" for an unmarried couple. We will examine the financial and tax consequences of this situation later in the book.

The Probate Process

The probate court (which has different names in different jurisdictions) enters the picture after an individual has died, when surviving family or friends initiate the procedure for transferring assets. If there is a will, the court will designate the *personal representative,* also called the *executor,* named in the will to manage the deceased's affairs. The personal representative locates all of the deceased's assets; pays his or her debts; engages attorneys, accountants, and other professionals as required; and finally distributes the assets and submits an accounting to the court to show where all the money went. If there is no will, the court will appoint someone to fulfill the personal representative's functions.

If the deceased owned real estate outside his or her home state, legal complications often require that a second probate proceeding, known as *ancillary probate,* be conducted in the other states where the real estate is situated. Ancillary probate can be expensive and time-consuming. We will return to this issue in Chapter Twelve.

General Elements of a Will

Although they are technical documents and contain their share of legal jargon, most wills are surprisingly readable—more so than, say, a lease for a new car. When your attorney drafts a will you should read it carefully and make certain it does exactly what you want it to do.

Usually a will starts by declaring the name of its maker, the *testator,* asserting that he or she is of sound mind, and declaring the state of domicile where the testator assumes the will is to be probated. (Occasionally, a will may be probated in another state, generally because the testator has moved since executing the document. Since state laws governing wills vary, it is a good idea to have an attorney in your new state review any existing will if you have moved since it was written.)

The testator should identify all living and adopted children, regardless of whether he (or she) intends to make a bequest to them under the will. A disinherited child's assertion that the testator merely overlooked him when the will was drafted can be defeated by this simple step.

The will may make certain *specific bequests.* The most common specific bequests are of the home (typically to the spouse or domestic partner); tangible personal property such as jewelry, artwork, and other personal effects (to a spouse, domestic partner, or children); and gifts of specific amounts of money, *pecuniary bequests,* to individuals or charities. Since there is a chance that the recipient of a specific bequest may not survive the testator, the will may provide for alternate recipients.

It is not unusual to find that property specifically bequeathed under a will was sold or otherwise disposed of by the testator after the will was drafted. This is called *ademption.* Unless otherwise provided in the will, the person who would have received the property gets nothing in its place.

A will may provide for the cancellation of certain debts that are owed to the decedent. This provision is really just another kind of specific bequest.

Probate property that is not subject to any specific bequests makes up the *residue* of the estate. The residue can easily comprise most or even all of the probate estate. The will describes who is to receive the residue; this recipient is the *residuary beneficiary.* The residue can be divided among more than one recipient under virtually any arrangement the testator cares to specify. In a typical situation, a mother's will might leave her jewelry to be divided equally among her children, while leaving everything else—the residue—to her surviving mate.

The will may establish one or more *testamentary trusts* instead of making certain bequests outright to the beneficiary. The will should specify the terms of the trust (when and to whom income and principal are to be distributed) and who will be the *trustee* responsible for managing the trust assets. There are many reasons for establishing testamentary trusts. One typical reason is to hold bequests that are for the benefit of children; such trusts may pay their principal to the child when he or she reaches adulthood or may keep the principal in trust until the child reaches a more seasoned age. Generally, the more money involved, the more reason there is to put it in trust and keep it there until a child has time to mature; there are very few eighteen- to twenty-one-year-olds who can deal responsibly with sudden access to money in the six-figure range and up. Other reasons for using testamentary trusts will be discussed in Chapter Twelve.

Many wills, especially for small and medium estates, waive the statutory requirements that personal representatives and trustees post a bond to protect the estate against misuse of its assets. Bonds cost money, and the theory for waiving the requirement is that if the testator has chosen trustworthy individuals to serve the estate, there is no need to incur the cost of the bond (which would be deducted from the estate's assets).

Naming Guardians for Children

A very important part of estate planning is the selection of guardians, trustees, and custodians. Guardians are required to provide for the care and upbringing of minor children and perhaps others, such as an infirm parent or a disabled adult child. Trustees and custodians take care of property for the benefit of those same individuals or others.

If you name a guardian in your will the probate court generally will respect your choice, but this is not automatic. Courts usually will award custody of minor children to a surviving natural or adoptive parent, regardless of the wishes of the deceased parent, unless there is evidence that the surviving parent is unfit. Even if there is no surviving parent, the court will consider whether placing a child with your chosen guardian is in the child's best interests.

If you want custody of your child to remain with your domestic partner, it is sometimes possible, and often very helpful, to arrange to have your partner legally adopt the child. Adoption can ward off a bitter court battle over custody if another relative decides to challenge your decision. Needless to say, if you and your partner have children together, you should be certain to select the same guardian in your wills; to do otherwise is virtually to guarantee the issue will be thrown into the lap of a judge.

Some attorneys recommend that you describe in a detailed separate letter attached to your will your reasons for selecting the guardian you chose. The more information you can give a judge about your child, your guardian, and the other potential guardians (and why you did not choose them), the better your chance of having a court enforce your decision.

You can name coguardians, but my advice is: Don't. Every time I have seen someone try this, I quickly discovered disagreement between the parents over who would make the best guardian. The coguardian approach may seem like a fair compromise, but in practice it creates a great risk of friction, litigation, and disruption of the children's lives. Remember, as long as you are alive and competent you can amend your will whenever you feel it is necessary. Work out the conflict now, rather than leave it to the survivors or the courts to resolve later.

Many parents will leave life insurance or other significant assets behind to provide for young children. The guardian you choose to rear the child may also be the perfect person to handle their money.

However, that's unlikely. The skills that make someone a fine surrogate parent do not necessarily make a good financial trustee, or vice versa. There is nothing wrong with separating custody of the *children* from custody of the *money*. In fact, it is often the wisest choice. Of course, the trustee needs to be given sufficient authority and flexibility to make good decisions about managing the money.

Providing for Parents and the Infirm

Not long ago I led a retirement planning seminar for a group of factory workers in Delaware. There were about twenty couples in the room, all between the ages of fifty-two and sixty. I asked everyone who had children in or approaching college to raise their hands; about half did. Then I asked everyone who had financial concerns about their elderly parents to raise their hands. Nearly every hand in the room went up.

Today's adults are the first generation to face the burden of providing for our parents, our children, and our own retirement all at the same time. It is a major financial-planning hurdle for many people and it also can be an estate-planning issue as well.

A large outright bequest to a parent often is not a good idea. If the parent is ill or incompetent, the assets may have to be spent in order for the parent to receive financial help through the Medicaid program. (Medicaid is the primary health-care funding mechanism for those without assets or insurance.) The recipient also may lack the skill or confidence to manage the money. Also, if the parent has funds independently or if your bequest is very large, you may trigger an unnecessary estate tax as assets are passed "up" a generation from you to your parents and eventually "down" again to your children or other heirs.

A better approach is to set up a trust (either while you are alive or through your will) to provide for your parents' needs and those of other beneficiaries. Properly structured, this trust can be outside your parents' estate and your own as well, can avoid affecting the parents' eligibility for Medicaid, and provide for money-management skill that your parents may lack.

If your parent is mentally competent you might suggest that he or she execute a durable power of attorney giving you or someone else the power to act on his or her behalf. An alternative, if your parent has significant wealth, might be to establish a revocable trust with you as trustee or cotrustee. This would allow you to step in and manage the parent's property in the event of a later disability.

If your parent is not mentally competent you could ask a court to appoint a guardian (or successor guardian if you currently fill that role), or you might put a provision in your will asking the court to appoint the guardian of your choice.

Disinheriting Your Partner

States make it difficult or impossible to disinherit a spouse. In community-property states, of course, the spouse is automatically a one-half owner of most property acquired during the marriage, unless that spouse has specifically agreed otherwise. All of the "common-law" states provide that a spouse has a right to receive at least a certain minimum share of a deceased mate's estate, regardless of will provisions or most nonprobate arrangements.

This protection is completely lacking for non-spouse domestic partners. In fact, the opposite is true: The non-spouse partner is automatically disinherited unless the deceased specifically provides otherwise through a will or non-probate property arrangement. Accidental disinheritance is one of the largest financial risks faced by unmarried domestic partners. Ignore this fact at your peril.

4

In Sickness, In Health

A family faces the loss of a loved one unless an organ donor can be found, an operation funded, an experimental cure provided. We have all heard these kinds of appeals, and who has *not* wanted to help?

You can learn much about a society's values by looking at who it tries to heal. Our health-care funding system is built around the traditional family. An employed worker (who is lucky enough to still receive comprehensive health benefits) can usually choose to cover himself or herself, a spouse, dependent children, or all of them. A family may buy private health insurance or may qualify for Medicaid. Only Medicare, which is provided on an individual basis, does not look to the family unit.

The unmarried domestic partner has no place in this picture. Very few private employers allow their workers to cover a non-spouse partner, and in the government and nonprofit sector the picture is only a little bit brighter. The unwed domestic partner is mostly left to fend for himself.

In this chapter we take a look at how the health and welfare benefit system in this country applies to unmarried couples. In the short term there are certain steps a couple can take to tailor or supplement existing benefits; in the long term, perhaps the ongoing

restructuring of our health-care system will make it more respon-
sive to individual needs. Although this chapter touches on various
insurance issues, an in-depth discussion of insurance products and
their applications is deferred to Chapter Eleven so that we can first
get a better understanding of related problems such as estate taxes.

Life Insurance

Life insurance is often one of the easiest financial-planning needs
that an unmarried couple can address. For most Americans, the
primary source of insurance is the workplace, especially employer-
provided "group term" policies that allow up to $50,000 of death
benefit to be paid for by the employer without any taxable income
being allocated to the covered employee. These programs often
provide benefits (either automatic or optional) well in excess of the
$50,000 level, with employees paying tax on the amount the em-
ployer spends to provide insurance in excess of $50,000.

In most employer-sponsored life insurance plans the employee
can designate anyone he or she wants as beneficiary (unlike, for
example, health plans, which are mainly restricted to spouses and
children.) If Paul is living with Paula, he can name her as beneficiary of his workplace life insurance coverage without any objection
from the employer or the insurer.

How much coverage should Paul provide for Paula? It depends
upon her situation. If Paula is capable of earning her own living and
does not rely on Paul for support, she may not need insurance on
Paul's life. On the other hand, if she wants to stay at home with
young children, and if she would inherit Paul's interest in their
home subject to a mortgage with a stiff monthly payment, she may
need a policy that is big enough to pay off the mortgage and still
provide her with sufficient funds to raise and educate the children.

Paul can always change his beneficiary designation in case the
couple's needs change or they break up. The only exception would
be if Paul irrevocably assigns the right to control his employer-

provided coverage (a strategy that Paul would use only if he has considerable wealth and wishes to avoid estate tax on the life insurance benefit).

If the employer-provided insurance is not enough to meet Paula's needs, Paul might seek to acquire insurance separately, or *Paula* might purchase a policy on Paul's life. The following worksheets will help you determine how much insurance you have and how much you need.

Disability Coverage

Disability insurance is probably one of the most overlooked, and tragic, areas of insurance planning for young people in general. An individual in his or her thirties has better than three times the chance of being disabled prior to age sixty-five as of dying in the same period. Yet most people pay much more attention to their life insurance coverage than to disability. Unmarried couples are particularly prone to problems.

If you are part of an unmarried couple you face a doubly complicated situation. First, you must consider what would happen if you became unable to work. If you are the primary earner in the household, could your partner make up the lost income? If you are not the primary earner, how much can you rely on support that your partner might provide?

In general, the wisest course is for each partner to maintain adequate disability coverage. "Adequate," in this case, generally means coverage that can replace 60% to 70% of pretax income.

There are exceptions, of course. The people who least need disability coverage are those who can rely on assets or income from some other source. Your own family's funds, or trusts that may have been established for your benefit, are possible sources of support. So may be the wealth of your partner—provided you have strong assurance that these funds will in fact be available to support you in

Insurance Summary

Name:

Part 1: Life Insurance

	Policy 1	Policy 2	Policy 3
Insurance Company			
Policy Number			
Insured			
Year Issued			
Face Amount			
Current Death Benefit (if different from face amount)			
Current Surrender (Cash) Value			
Annual Premium			
Total Premiums Paid to Date			
Premium Expected to Be Paid Through Year _____ (see Note A)			
Policy Loans Outstanding			
Interest Rate on Policy Loans			
Policy Owner			
Primary Beneficiary(ies)			
Contingent Beneficiary(ies)			
Dividend Option (see Note B)			

NOTES:

(A): If premiums are expected to be paid for life, indicate "life." If a premium "vanish" is expected, indicate the last year cash premiums are expected to be due for each policy. Note that premium vanish years can differ from initial sales projections due to changes in insurance company charges and dividends.

(B): Typical dividend options are to be paid in cash, to reduce premiums, to purchase additional paid-up insurance (PUAs), or to be deposited in an interest-bearing account with the insurance company.

Life Insurance Requirements

Name:

Cash Required at Death

Funeral _____
Estate administration _____
Estate taxes _____
Emergency fund for family expenses _____
Current bills _____
Total _____

Cash Available at Death

Insurance proceeds _____
Death benefits of retirement programs _____
Liquid assets _____
Other
Total _____

Net Cash Available (or Required) at Death

_____

Assets Available for Mortgage and Children's Education

Mortgage outstanding _____
Education (see Note A) _____
Total _____

Assets Available for Mortgage and Children's Education

Investment assets _____
Personal assets convertible to cash _____
Other _____
Total _____

Net Assets Available (Required) for Mortgage and Education

_____

Survivor Living Expenses (Note B)

_____

Income Available for Survivor Living Expenses

Income from assets _____
Employment income of survivor(s) _____
Other _____
Total _____

Annual Income Excess (or Deficiency)

_____

Additional Insurance Required

Cash required at death _____
Mortgage and education _____
Living expenses _____
_____

NOTES:

(A): This is the amount which, if invested today, would grow to a sum sufficient to provide the desired contribution to children's educational expenses.

(B): This is the amount which, if invested today, would provide an income stream to surviving domestic partner, children, or other beneficiaries for the desired length of time.

time of need. Remember, unless you have a strong and enforceable legal agreement with your partner, there is little to stop him or her from simply terminating the relationship if you become a financial or emotional burden.

Unfortunately, most of us cannot obtain disability coverage either for our spouses or domestic partners through the workplace; most employer-sponsored disability programs cover employees only. You will have to turn to the private insurance market for coverage in most cases. There, you will find the policy costs and provisions vary widely, as we will consider shortly. A worksheet to summarize and evaluate disability coverage is provided on the following page. You should address your disability situation as soon as you become self-supporting, whenever you change jobs, or at least once every two years.

How Disability Insurance Works

Disability insurance protects against *long-term loss of income* resulting from illness or injury. That simple-sounding definition hides a great deal of complexity. Disability insurance products vary widely in cost and scope of coverage. Further complicating the disability insurance issue is the fact that many workers are eligible for Social Security disability (but only after you have worked for at least one-and-a-half years or more, depending upon your age when you become disabled) or, if the disability results from employment, Worker's Compensation.

For most people, the first and often the only source of disability protection is what is made available through their employer. Employers may offer disability coverage in conjunction with sick leave (short-term disability pay that is usually paid by the employer itself rather than an insurance company). Sometimes the employer pays the premium, sometimes the employee pays, and sometimes the employee has the option of whether to sign up (and pay for) the coverage.

If the employer pays for disability coverage, any benefits received by the employee will be subject to income tax. If the em-

Insurance Summary

Name:

Part 2: Disability

	Policy 1	Policy 2	Policy 3
Insurance Company	_____	_____	_____
Policy Number	_____	_____	_____
Insured	_____	_____	_____
Year Issued	_____	_____	_____
Annual Premium	_____	_____	_____
Monthly Benefit	_____	_____	_____
Definition of Disability (see Note A)	_____	_____	_____
Waiting (Elimination) Period	_____	_____	_____
Benefit Period (see Note B)	_____	_____	_____
Cost-of-Living Adjustment	_____	_____	_____
Guaranteed Renewable	_____	_____	_____
Partial Disability Coverage	_____	_____	_____
Residual Disability Coverage	_____	_____	_____
Retraining Benefits	_____	_____	_____

NOTES:

(A): Usual definitions of disability provide benefits when insured cannot perform duties of: 1) own occupation; 2) any occupation for which he/she is reasonably suited by training and experience; 3) any occupation; 4) some combination of above (e.g. #1 for first two years, #3 thereafter).

(B): Benefits under disability policies are payable until death, until age 65, or for a shorter period as provided under the policy.

ployee pays, any benefits received are tax-free, and this is true even if the payments are actually made by the employer out of deductions from the employee's pay. As noted earlier, most people should seek an aftertax (or tax-free) benefit of 60% to 70% of salary in order to maintain approximately the same living standard.

Some of the key considerations in selecting a disability plan include:

✓ **Definition of disability.** Some plans require only that your disability prevent you from performing your regular occupation. Others will only pay benefits if you cannot perform *any* gainful employment, while a few use vague compromise language like "any reasonable employment." *Split plans* pay benefits for a limited period of time (often two years) if you cannot perform the tasks of your own occupation, but continue to pay thereafter only if you cannot perform any gainful employment.

✓ **Duration of benefits.** Some plans will pay benefits only up to a certain number of years, others pay until age sixty-five, others for a lifetime. All, of course, pay only while the insured remains disabled.

✓ **Waiting period.** Virtually all disability plans require a waiting period between the onset of disability and the beginning of benefits. This waiting, or *elimination* period, is a kind of deductible. The longer the waiting period, the lower the policy premiums will be. Since most people maintain (or should maintain) an emergency fund of three to six months' expenses, most financial planners recommend an elimination period of at least ninety days. If you can afford to self-insure for longer periods, you can save on premiums by opting for a longer waiting period.

✓ **Cost-of-living adjustment.** An individual who suffers a permanent disability at age thirty will face decades of inflation that diminishes the value of his (or her) insurance benefit. Some plans incorporate a cost-of-living adjustment to compensate. This feature does raise the premium, but it is worthwhile protection unless you own other assets (such as real estate, stocks, etc.) that might offer a sufficient inflation hedge.

✓ **Guaranteed renewability.** Some disabling injuries are chronic and tend to recur; back injuries are one example. Certain policies give the insurer the right to cancel coverage after the first disability claim. If your coverage is cancelled, you will have a difficult time getting new insurance, since you will already have a history of disabling health problems. To provide real protection, the policy should specify that once it is issued it will automatically be renewed regardless of your future health, as long as you pay the premiums.

✓ **Additional purchase option.** Most workers expect their income to rise steadily over the course of their careers. Disability insurance that may be perfectly adequate today might be insufficient to maintain your living standard based on the income you will be earning five or ten years from now. An additional purchase option gives the insured the right to purchase additional insurance at some point in the future *without having to submit new evidence of good health at that time.*

✓ **Residual benefits.** Someone who has been disabled will often be able to return to work on a limited basis but not full-time. The better disability policies encourage this by providing for partial benefits to supplement these part-time earnings following total disability.

✓ **Rehabilitation benefits.** Most people would rather work than sit around the house. Insurance companies want to minimize the amount they pay to support someone who is not working. Some policies support these mutually consistent goals by providing funds for

rehabilitation training and treatment to help disabled
policyholders return to work.

Employer-sponsored disability programs contain varying mix-
tures of these features. A few companies offer *wrap* or supplemental policies to upgrade an employer's plan. For example, if your
employer's plan uses "any gainful employment" as the definition of
disability and you want "own occupation" coverage, you might buy
a wrap policy that will take over the payments in the event your
employer's plan ceases them under the "any gainful employment"
test.

Insurance companies will be leery of issuing disability policies
for much more than 60% of an individual's income, out of fear that
policyholders will begin to fake disabilities if it is financially advantageous for them to do so. However, in a few situations, coverage
will be approved for higher amounts.

Employee Benefits

Every once in a while some well-meaning legislator tries to repeal
unenforced statutes, such as criminal laws against homosexual conduct. Often these efforts fail amid protests by other lawmakers that
since these laws are not used to hurt anyone, there is no reason to
stir up a political hornet's nest by repealing them.

These laws can indeed hurt in unintended ways. One example is
in the taxation of employee benefits. Suppose, for example, you
work for a progressive employer who extends health benefits to
non-spouse domestic partners. While these benefits are normally
tax-free when provided to family members and other dependents,
the Internal Revenue Code makes the benefit taxable if "the relationship . . . is in violation of local law."* In practice this is mainly
an academic problem, since it is rare that the IRS actually asserts

---

* I.R.C. Sec. 152(b) (5).

this position, but the existence of these provisions creates a tax trap both for employees who may be subject to tax and employers who may be responsible for withholding it.

On a brighter note, a small but growing number of employers and localities are recognizing non-marital domestic relationships. Late in 1992, for example, Stanford University and the University of Chicago extended health insurance, tuition breaks, library privileges, and other benefits to gay and lesbian domestic partners. (Note that unmarried heterosexual partners are not included, presumably because marriage is usually an option for those people.)

New York City began registering domestic partners in March 1993. Those who work for the city are granted the same unpaid leave that married workers receive to care for a new child in the household, and are granted the same visiting privileges that spouses are given at city hospitals and prisons. More importantly, in a city where more people rent than own their homes, the city's rent-control laws were extended to give domestic partners the same rights as spouses in retaining possession following the death of the lessee.

All told, about twenty-five localities across the nation grant some recognition to domestic partners, according to recent press reports.

Health Insurance

The cost of health care played a major role in the 1992 presidential election, helping to bring to office an administration that pledged to revamp a system that leaves millions of people exposed to financial disaster while providing only haphazard access to care. The Clinton reform proposals would create a system of universal health insurance financed primarily by the nation's employers and containing new mechanisms to control costs.

In some respects the Clinton proposals are just a further evolution of the current situation. Private employers have for decades taken the lead in providing access to health care through company-sponsored benefits. Since the 1960s government has become deeply involved through the Medicaid program, which provides care to financially strapped families, and Medicare, an extension of Social Security that focuses on providing care for the elderly.

Unfortunately, most employer-sponsored programs ignore the presence of unmarried domestic partners, leaving this group disproportionately represented among Americans who lack medical insurance. The situation has been changing, but only very slowly. Some municipalities and colleges, and a few companies, have begun offering employees an opportunity to acquire coverage for domestic partners. Those that have tried it have reported that costs are small and benefits, in the form of improved morale and employee loyalty, can be large. In some cases, only same-sex domestic partners are granted coverage, on grounds that opposite-sex couples could be legally wed if they want formal recognition of their status.

But widespread acceptance of domestic-partner benefits may not happen any time soon. In the first place, religious and political opposition in many areas of the country make it difficult for politicians and academics (especially in government- and religious-funded institutions) who will not want to be seen as "endorsing" an "alternative lifestyle." (Witness the recent controversy when a Texas county withheld tax breaks from Apple Computer to protest the company's provision of health benefits to domestic partners. The county commission ultimately reversed itself and offered the breaks to Apple, but only after drawing national attention to the local hostility toward gay and other unconventional couples.)

Second, even the jurisdictions that have attempted to guarantee equal rights for homosexuals or that allow registration of domestic partners have stopped well short of mandating that private employers provide equal benefits. A tough economy gives employers great leverage in threatening to take their jobs elsewhere, and concern is already high that the cost of providing health benefits makes U.S. companies uncompetitive in world markets.

The best many people can do is try to obtain private coverage, perhaps through a Health Maintenance Organization (HMO), until such time as our nation truly provides universal access to affordable, quality health care. In the meantime, the worksheet on the following page will help you identify and evaluate your current coverage.

When a Partner Is Incapacitated

So far in this chapter we have considered the financial side of illness, injury, and death. Now it is time to look at the emotional and legal side, the ways in which we can cope with the incapacity of a partner.

Fortunately, the law here is not quite so biased against unmarried couples. True, in many areas there are judges, doctors, and other interested parties who do not place appropriate value on a long-term committed relationship. But there is a good selection of tools that force society to recognize the unmarried couple's unique facts of life. Let's look at a hypothetical situation.

Insurance Summary

Name:

Part 3: Medical

	Policy 1	Policy 2	Policy 3
Insured Person(s)			
Insurance Company			
HMO, PPO, or Other "Managed Care"?			
Group Policy/Program?			
Annual Premium			
Authorization Required for Emergency Treatment? (if yes, give telephone number)			
Authorization Required For Non-Emergency Treatment? (if yes, give telephone number)			
Major Medical (except HMOs):			
Annual Limit—Individual			
Annual Limit—Family			
Deductible—Individual			
Deductible—Family			
Lifetime Limit—Individual			
Lifetime Limit—Family			
Co-Payment Percentage			
Co-Payment Applies to First $$?			
Hospitalization (except HMOs):			
Daily Room Charge Covered			
Maximum Number of Days			
Maximum Other Expenses (except surgery)			
Maximum Surgical Expense			

▪ CASE 1: The Well-Prepared Partner

Karen's parents were shocked and very upset when she told them she was a lesbian. Raised in a religious southern Indiana household, Karen had denied her own sexuality all through high school, dating many boys and sleeping with a few. She had her first homosexual experience with a college classmate during her sophomore year. Still, she tried to fit the image her family had of her, marrying at the end of her senior year.

Just a few years later Karen knew that she would never be happy in her marriage. She had finished business school by then and had taken a good job on Wall Street. She divorced Ken and, a few months later, began living with Dana, an artist. A month later Karen took a week's vacation, alone, to go back to Indiana and break the news to her parents.

They offered to pay for religious or psychological counseling, but Karen said she was perfectly happy and did not need it. For the remaining four days of her visit Karen scarcely spoke to her parents. They asked her not to return home for Christmas that year; she made plans to go to Dana's family home in Boston instead.

A week before Christmas Karen was in a car crash that left her paralyzed from the neck down. Her firm's medical and disability coverage took care of the out-of-pocket costs and paid for physical therapy. Five weeks later Karen was out of the hospital and home with Dana, who took excellent care of her.

Karen's parents filed suit seeking legal guardianship of their daughter. They maintained that Karen's present condition of dependence upon Dana left her unable to render an independent judgment as to the best party to take care of her.

At a hearing two weeks later a judge expressed sympathy for the parents' position, until Dana's attorney produced a power of attorney Karen had executed three months before the accident. In that document Karen had given Dana complete control of her financial as well as medical affairs. The power of attorney proved that Karen had wanted Dana all along to be the person to care for her in the event of incapacity. The judge agreed and dismissed Karen's parents' lawsuit.

Karen's use of a simple document—the durable power of attorney—was enough to spare her untold grief and also prevented a legal battle between her parents and Dana which might well have led to permanent estrangement. A power of attorney may prove to be the most important document an unmarried domestic partner ever signs. It deserves a closer look.

Durable Power of Attorney

A power of attorney is a straightforward legal document in which one person, the *principal,* appoints another person, the *agent* or *attorney-in-fact,* to conduct certain of the principal's affairs. Many of us have signed a power of attorney giving someone the power to sign for us at a closing or to represent us at a hearing.

In traditional agency law, an agent retains the power to act only as long as the principal does not revoke his (or her) authority. Under this concept the agent loses his or her authority immediately if the principal dies or becomes mentally incompetent, since it is no longer clear that the principal would wish the agent to have his powers.

A *durable* power of attorney is special because it allows the agent to continue representing the principal after the principal has become incompetent. (The principal must, of course, be competent when he initially signs the durable power.) If you hold or have signed a power of attorney but don't know whether it is durable, take a look at it. It will either contain the words "durable power" or it will have language to the effect that "this power shall survive and remain in force notwithstanding the physical or mental condition" of the principal. If it does not contain this sort of language, it will not be enforceable if you become incompetent. Note that no power of attorney is valid once the principal is dead; the estate's personal representative assumes the agent's powers.

A power of attorney can be very broad, giving the power holder the right to do virtually any legal act that the principal could do, or it can be very narrow. Generally, a durable power is effective immediately upon signing. Some people who want their power holder to be able to act only after they have become incompetent are more comfortable using a special type of durable power known as a *springing power of attorney.*

The springing power becomes effective only when the maker is incompetent. The power springs into action, so to speak, upon the occurrence of that contingency. How is incompetence determined? Usually, the document itself will name two or three doctors (chosen in advance by the principal) whose written opinion is sufficient; this avoids the need for a court proceeding to determine incompetence. A fringe benefit is privacy: Court proceedings to determine someone's incompetence and appoint guardians are generally public, while a power of attorney operates in private.

A health-care power of attorney is a specialized durable power that deals only with health-care issues. Most often people grant this power to their spouse or domestic partner, trusting this person to make the best decisions about the course of medical treatment in extreme circumstances. A health-care power can replace or supplement a *living will,* which is the individual's own expression of his desires concerning treatment. A health-care power can cover a wide range of situations in which the principal cannot speak for himself, while the living will is generally effective only in the last stages of a terminal illness.

If you become incompetent without having granted a durable power of attorney, chances are that a close relative or domestic partner will have to go to court to win powers to assist you. This approach has many hazards. If your loved ones wait too long, your financial and personal affairs can fall into serious disarray. If they disagree about who should handle your affairs, a judge may have to play umpire in a nasty confrontation. Even if all goes well, the court proceeding will entail delays and costs that could have been avoided, and because the choice is at the judge's discretion, your affairs may not be placed in the hands of the person you would prefer.

A court can appoint a *guardian* to serve as the personal care-taker and legal spokesperson for the disabled individual, if that person is unable to express his or her own views competently, as well as a *conservator* to manage the disabled person's property. The conservator will manage the individual's property under the court's guidelines and supervision, in much the same way as the trustee of a trust.

These court procedures are an important and necessary safe-guard, but good planning means you should never have to use them. It is better always to keep a durable power of attorney in effect. Not only is this action likely to head off a court battle, it provides a clear statement of the disabled person's own wishes, which itself may avoid much grief and bad feeling.

5

An Investment Program

Interest rates are down. The certificate of deposit is about to mature. Please, Ms. Financial Planner, what should I invest in?

Sometimes financial planners feel that everyone who attends a cocktail party is duty-bound to ask this question. If you have tortured a financial professional this way, shame on you. How should *she* know what you should invest in? You have not told her what you are investing *for*. Or how much you want to invest. Or how large your other investments are. Or how willing (and able) you are to withstand a loss, either actual or on paper. Or anything else about yourself, your goals, and your fears.

Investing is the most complex financial decision most people make. There are countless books, articles, and seminars on the topic, and nearly as many advisors, salespeople, and flat-out con artists, all ready (notwithstanding their own ignorance) to tell you what to do with your money. Even with all this alleged help available, most people make terrible investment decisions.

This chapter will focus on the whys and wherefores of investing from the point of view of the unmarried couple, a relationship that adds some unique complications to the usual challenges of successful investing.

The Basics

For all its complexity, investing really is just the practical application of some very simple concepts. These include:

✓ As rewards (investment returns) increase, so does risk.

✓ A particular type of investment, such as stocks or bonds, tends to have very stable performance relative to other types of investments when viewed over long periods of time. Stocks, for example, historically return more than twice as much as bonds. Short periods of time are quite another story. Some investments are prone to wider swings in value than others, so in the short run there is no way to predict which investment will yield the best return.

✓ Investment principles operate *in the aggregate*—over large numbers of individual stocks, over long periods of time, and over large numbers of investors. Results can be very different when individual units, such as particular stocks or portfolios, are examined.

We can turn personal investing (building up a "nest egg") into a little equation:

$$\textbf{Nest Egg = (Capital Invested + Time Invested)} \\ \textbf{$\times$ Risk Taken}$$

Take twice as much risk, get twice as much reward. Invest money longer, or invest more of it, and you end up with more. This equation is too simple to satisfy the economists, but it works for our purposes.

Be careful. In the world of investing you can never get something for nothing. When somebody offers you more return, they are generally asking you to accept more risk. If an opportunity sounds too good to be true, place your hand on your wallet and squeeze tightly.

Establishing Goals

As I briefly mentioned in Chapter Two, good financial planning begins with goal-setting. Using your Net Worth Statement as a starting point and your goals as a desired destination, you can map out an investment strategy that gets you where you want to go without unnecessary risk.

Risk and return are so closely linked that, beyond a certain point, it is impossible to increase an investment portfolio's return without increasing risk. Let's assume that you are a normal investor who wants to take only as much risk as is necessary to meet your goal. Let us further assume that your goal is to accumulate $100,000 by the time your child enters college ten years from now and that you already have accumulated $40,000. Plugging the numbers into a financial calculator tells us that you will need a return of just under 9.6%, compounded annually, to meet your goal. If somebody offers you an investment that projects an 11% return, you might reject it, on the grounds that the investment carries more risk than you need to take in order to achieve your minimum desired return of 9.6%.

By setting your investment goal up front, you have armed yourself with the knowledge to reject an inappropriate investment. An individual who had not bothered to figure out the amount required in ten years (or the rate of return required to earn it) might take the high-risk 11% investment, ignoring the risk and figuring that a little extra return cannot hurt.

Financial goals can be divided into short term, intermediate term, and long term. These periods are known as the *time horizon*. As the time horizon lengthens, the amount of investment risk you can afford to take on will increase. This means that, on average, we expect long-term investments to perform better than short-term investments. The table below examines a set of typical financial planning goals for a thirty-five-year-old parent with one small child.

Most of us have goals that fall into more than one time frame, as is the case with the young parent illustrated above. This dilemma forces us to make trade-offs. Unfortunately, most of the time the trade-offs follow a pattern: Intermediate goals take priority over long-term goals, short-term goals take precedence over intermediate goals, and current spending needs (like the new home entertainment center we just *cannot* live without) jump in front of short-term goals. Unless we discipline ourselves, the long term may arrive only to find us unprepared. The worksheet on pages 70–71 will help you identify and set priorities among your financial goals.

Time Horizon	Financial Goals	Typical Investments	Desired Behavior
Short Term (under 2 years)	Purchase car; establish emergency fund	Bank accounts; money market funds; short-term bond funds; Treasury bills	Stability of principal (minimal price swings); safety; ready access; easy regular additions
Intermediate Term (2–10 years)	Buy home	Growth and income stocks; intermediate- and long-term bonds; mutual funds	Higher growth; diversification
Long term (over 10 years)	Child's college; retirement	Small-company stocks; aggressive-growth mutual funds; life insurance and annuity products; real estate; precious metals; collectibles	Highest growth (consistent with financial requirements and risk tolerance); diversification; inflation protection

Financial Goals Worksheet

Name:

Date:

Step 1: Identify and Classify Financial Objectives

For each of the following financial objectives, identify its importance to you (high, medium, low, none), and indicate whether achieving the objective is a short-term goal (within 2 years), medium-term (2–10 years), or long-term (more than 10 years).

Objective	Term	IMPORTANCE High	Medium	Low	None
Spending & Lifestyle					
Improve Present Standard of Living (spending)					
Improve Future Standard of Living (spending)					
Financial Independence at Age ___					
Retirement at Age ___					
New Home					
Vacation Home					
New Car/Truck					
New Boat, Airplane, Other Vehicle					
Extensive Travel					
Weddings, Bar Mitzvah, Other Large Affair					
Other					
Dependent Support					
Own Education (college, grad school, trade school, etc.)					
Children's Education					
Support Elderly Parents					
Support Domestic Partner					
Gifts to Loved Ones					
Gifts to Charity					
Other					
Saving & Investment					
Build Financial Cushion					
Build Retirement Fund					
Change Career					
Start Business					
Other					

Financial Goals Worksheet

Step 2: Organize Goals by Time Horizon

In this section you should list the goals you established in Part 1. Put each goal in the appropriate time horizon and list them in order of priority, beginning with the most important.

	IMPORTANCE		
	High	Medium	Low
Short-Term Goals			
_____	____	____	____
_____	____	____	____
_____	____	____	____
_____	____	____	____
_____	____	____	____
_____	____	____	____
_____	____	____	____
_____	____	____	____
_____	____	____	____
Medium-Term Goals			
_____	____	____	____
_____	____	____	____
_____	____	____	____
_____	____	____	____
_____	____	____	____
_____	____	____	____
_____	____	____	____
_____	____	____	____
Long-Term Goals			
_____	____	____	____
_____	____	____	____
_____	____	____	____
_____	____	____	____
_____	____	____	____
_____	____	____	____
_____	____	____	____

Financial Goals Worksheet

Step 3: Compute Funds for Goals

NOTE: To complete these calculations you will need a financial calculator, a personal computer, or a hand-held calculator and separate tables of future and present values of $1 and future value of an annuity in advance (an "annuity due").

This worksheet allows you to compute the funding required to meet each financial goal under one of two methods: 1) A lump sum, invested today; 2) a series of periodic (annual) investments.

1. Financial Goal: _____

2. Current Savings for Goal: _____

3. Estimated Cost (current dollars): _____

4. Number of Years to Reach Goal: _____

5. Estimated Future Inflation: _____

6. Estimated Aftertax Return on Investments: _____

Computation of Lump-Sum Amount

Lump-Sum Required = (PV $1, at estimated aftertax return on investments, for number of years to reach goal)

_____

Future Cost of Goal = (Estimated cost in current dollars) x (FV $1, at estimated future inflation rate, for number of years to reach goal)

_____

Subtract Future Cost from Lump Sum. This is the additional amount you should invest today to achieve the specified goal.

_____

Computation of Required Annual Contribution

Future Value of Current Savings = (Current savings) x (FV $1, at estimated aftertax return on investments, for number of years to reach goal)

_____

Future Cost of Goal = (Estimated cost in current dollars) x (FV $1, at estimated future inflation rate, for number of years to reach goal)

_____

Amount to be Saved Through Annual Contributions = (Future Cost - Future Value of Current Savings)

_____

Required Annual Contribution = (Amount to be saved) / (FVA , at estimated aftertax return on investments, for number of years to goal)

_____

Working Together

By now you are starting to see that successful investing will require clarity of purpose, steady nerves, patience, and self-discipline. When couples are planning their financial future it also requires teamwork.

The basic question boils down to this: How permanent is the relationship? Or, as we put it in Chapter Two, are we Newly (Un)Weds, a Committed Couple, or something else? The wrong answer to this question can have disastrous consequences, as illustrated in the following hypothetical case.

♟ CASE 1: Roger, Over and Out

Roger was an experienced pilot for a major airline. From his base in Orlando, Florida, he flew routes that regularly brought him to New York, Chicago, and the West Coast. The job came with plenty of time off and, of course, ample opportunity to travel.

Sheri met Roger during one of his New York stopovers in 1985. Then widowed with a one-year-old son, she wanted to get married again. But Roger said they should wait until the airline's financial picture improved and he could arrange a transfer or, even better, a management job in New York, where Sheri wanted to remain to avoid separating her son from his paternal grandparents. The years passed and Roger's financially strapped employer repeatedly denied his request for a transfer.

Roger continued to save for their future. He put aside $15,000 annually in his company-sponsored retirement plan, and another $8,000 per year toward their eventual purchase of a home. Invested in a growth-stock mutual fund, the new-home kitty had reached $125,000 by late 1992. Sheri had a good management job but she earned much less than Roger. She paid for their home in New York as well as the hotels and other out-of-pocket costs of frequent vacations, while Roger provided the low-cost transportation and put his money away.

In 1992 Roger met Janet, a theme-park executive in Orlando. Just six weeks later he flew to New York to tell Sheri he was going to marry Janet. Using the money he had put aside, Roger and Janet were wed in an elaborate ceremony and bought a comfortable home in an Orlando suburb.

Sheri found herself without any substantial savings, and with a child who, by 1992, was only about ten years away from college. Had she and Roger been married, Sheri would have been entitled to equitable distribution, including a share of Roger's retirement plan. But, as an unmarried partner, she had no recourse.

Under the circumstances Sheri felt she had been foolish to rely on Roger's promises for the financial security of herself and her son. While she paid for their ongoing expenses, he put extra money away for his own future.

What does the case of Roger and Sheri teach us? First, in many instances—probably the majority—each partner should bear a fair share of the current spending, and thus have an opportunity to save and invest in his or her own account. Alternatively, the investments could be made in a joint account subject to an agreement that would give each partner a share in the event of a breakup. Such an arrangement is not possible with most retirement plans, however. When most of the saving is being done through such a plan, the parties will have to work out other ways of keeping the score relatively even. We will cover retirement plans in more detail in Chapter Seven. For now let's take a look at the role these plans play in our savings and investment programs.

Retirement Plans

Earlier in this century the employer-sponsored retirement plan became part of our social safety net. These early plans were called *defined benefit* plans because they paid a fixed benefit for the life of the employee (and sometimes his surviving beneficiary). The fixed pension benefit was usually computed as a fraction of final salary, with the biggest payments going to employees who had been with the employer the longest.

Great changes were reshaping the country's work force by the time the 1970s began. Workers seldom spent entire careers with one employer; they wanted "portable" retirement benefits that would follow them to new jobs (and new cities). Congress in 1974 enacted the Employee Retirement Income Security Act (ERISA), which thoroughly overhauled the nation's pension rules. One of ERISA's most important changes was to ban, after a transition period, "pay-as-you-go" pensions in which employers would promise benefits to today's workers but would only fund those benefits from tomorrow's earnings. The problem with pay-as-you-go, of course, is that if the employer has no earnings tomorrow, retirees can find themselves without pensions. ERISA established a new federal agency, the Pension Benefit Guaranty Corporation, to deal with that problem.

Now that employers were required to pay in advance for the pension benefits they promised, they faced a problem: how to invest the money. After all, if the investment did not work out, the employer was still responsible for paying the promised pension benefit. From the employee point of view, defined benefit plans had other drawbacks. Employees who frequently changed jobs might accrue little benefit since these plans are generally not "portable." And if the funds were invested too conservatively, the employee's retirement fund might not grow as well as it should.

With both employers and employees becoming disenchanted

with defined benefit plans, a solution had to be found. One was the *defined contribution* plan, most often structured as a "profit-sharing" arrangement that did not require employers to make any minimum contribution at all. Each employee was given a separate account in the retirement program. Employer contributions together with employee contributions (most prominently, salary reductions under "401(k)" plans) were earmarked for each employee individually. Often the employee was given a range of choices in how those funds were to be invested: stock funds, bond funds, money market funds, "guaranteed investment contracts" which basically were loans to insurance companies, and others. The size of the employee's retirement fund would depend largely on the investment decisions he (or she) made rather than on any promise by the employer. If an employee changed jobs he could often transfer his retirement account to his new employer's plan, "roll over" the amount to a personal account (the Individual Retirement Account or IRA), or sometimes just leave it in the old plan.

Generous tax incentives fed the explosive growth of the new plans, as they had earlier fed the growth of defined benefit plans. For many households, retirement accounts became either the largest asset or the second largest (behind the family residence), and was often the only significant asset that was readily convertible to cash.

By 1984 Congress confronted another problem: Spouses were not getting their fair share of the retirement pot. One situation of particular concern was the ability of the breadwinner to take a generous pension that would stop upon his death, leaving a surviving spouse with no income beyond Social Security survivor's benefits. Another problem was the inability of courts to divide fairly the retirement plan assets in divorce cases.

Congress responded with the Retirement Equity Act, which greatly strengthened the rights of spouses to the retirement plans of their partners. Spouses were automatically entitled to a survivor's pension equal to at least 50% of the amount received by the employed spouse. Courts were given leeway to divide the retirement assets under Qualified Domestic Relations Orders (QDROs).

This law provided significant protection to married, non-working individuals (or working individuals whose own employers did not provide them with a retirement plan). Unfortunately, it did nothing for unmarried domestic partners.

All the problems Congress sought to address for spouses continue to plague unmarried individuals. A domestic partner can elect a single life pension (and, in many plans, will automatically receive one unless the partner elects otherwise) regardless of the needs of the prospective surviving partner. Rules that prevent creditors from attacking an individual's pensions make retirement plans nearly invulnerable to assault by soon-to-be-ex domestic partners, who lack the special mechanism of the QDRO to get a fair share.

This brings us back to the role of the retirement plan in our personal investment strategy. For the most part, workers have no control over the investment of defined benefit plans. The employee works; the employer puts aside and invests enough money to pay the promised benefit once the employee retires.

Defined contribution plans, on the other hand, offer a wealth of investment possibilities. Employee accounts in these plans can be invested for long-term growth, they can be invested in very conservative money market instruments, and often they can also be invested in the stock of the employer. This latter approach carries great financial risk, because if the employer runs into financial trouble the employee may find both his or her job and retirement fund in jeopardy.

If one member of an unmarried couple has a large retirement fund, or the opportunity to amass a large fund, the other member must realize that ensuring a share of this money is difficult or impossible. Only the most stable and committed relationships can handle this problem without some attempt to achieve balance. In other domestic couples, the partner who does not benefit from the retirement plan growth had best consider how to protect himself or herself in the event the couple later separates. He or she should seize opportunities to save some money independently. Because of the tax advantages, an employer-sponsored plan or Individual Retirement Account is the best place to start (if the second partner also works). Other possibilities include permanent life insurance policies and annuities (both of which are discussed in Chapter Eleven), mutual funds, and real estate (such as owning the home the couple lives in).

The Investment Pyramid

Financial planners like to describe an investment "pyramid" that puts the stable, short-term investments on the bottom to provide a financial base, with increasingly long-term and risky investments as you move toward the top of the pyramid. A typical investment pyramid is shown in Figure 1.

Investment Pyramid Showing Increasing Risk, Returns

With married couples and parent-child situations I usually advise that the family's investment portfolios be combined so that we can view them as one large pyramid. In these cases, the older family members who are simply looking for stability and income should hold the stable, income-producing investments at the bottom of the pyramid, such as money market funds, while younger members who are more growth-oriented and risk-tolerant would hold the more volatile investments, such as small-company stocks that are near the top of the pyramid.

But what about unmarried couples? The potential instability of the relationship, combined with the lack of equitable distribution and other legal protection, makes it risky for one member to hold the growth investments and the other the stable, income-producing base assets. It is often desirable to try to give each member his or her own pyramid with a mix of stable and growth investments that would be appropriate in the event this individual has to go it alone.

Owning versus Lending

For all the noise about reverse repos, mortgage-backed securities, and other esoteric investment vehicles, there really are only two basic types of investments in the world. In one case, the investor is an *owner;* these are called *equities.* In the other, the investor is a *lender;* these are called *debts,* or *fixed-income* investments. The difference is huge.

Debt investments include bank deposits (which are just loans of your money to the bank); bonds; Treasury bills; mortgages; annuities and the like. In a debt, the investor (who is also the lender) is promised that he (or she) will receive his investment ("principal") at a certain point in time, together with compensation for the use of his money ("interest").

The *equity investor* owns part or all of something. If the something is a corporation, he or she owns shares of stock. If it is real estate, it may be all or a fractional interest of a building or land. It can be livestock, computers, or works of art. Virtually anything that can be owned can be the object of an equity investment.

Let's illustrate the difference between owning and lending.

⚑ CASE 2: Lend Me $1 Million

Smith and Jones were standing on the sidewalk one day, looking up at a shiny new office building that had a sign in the window: For Sale, $1 Million Cash.

"Sure wish I had a million dollars right now," Smith remarked. "I think this building is going to be worth $2 million a year from now. But all my money is tied up in a business deal that won't be settled for another six months."

"Not to worry," replied Jones. "I don't know that I share your opinion of this building, but I know you to be a successful businessman and a good credit risk. What say I lend you the million? At, say, 9%? A year from now you just pay me $1,090,000."

"Done," said Smith, and they hurried off to find the building's owner.

A year later Smith did, indeed, sell the building for $2 million. He paid Jones the $1,090,000 he owed him and kept the rest of the profit, a tidy $910,000 for which he had not had to put up a dime of his own funds.

In this case, Jones the lender invested in a debt instrument, namely, the mortgage on the building that Smith gave him. Smith was the equity investor.

Were the results of the transaction equal? Hardly. The building's value increased 100%, with 91% of the increase going to Smith the owner and only 9% to Jones the lender. Why would Jones enter into such a bad deal?

Well, Jones only got 9%, but it was the *first* 9% of the building's appreciation. If the building's value had only increased 9% over the year, the entire increase would have belonged to Jones. In fact, if the value had *dropped* by 9%, Jones would have been entitled to his $1,090,000, and Smith would have had to pay $180,000 of that out of his own pocket. So Smith accepted a bigger risk than Jones, and accordingly stood to receive a larger return.

Many economists have studied the historical risks (fluctuations in value) and returns (interest, dividends, and capital appreciation) of different types of investments. The numbers vary slightly depending upon the exact investments and periods under study, but the pattern is remarkably consistent: In the United States, equity investments such as stock and real estate have tended to provide approximately twice the return of debt investments, such as corporate and government bonds. When favorable tax treatment for capital gains is taken into account, the results in favor of equities are even better.

But these better returns come, as we would expect, at substantially higher risk. The stock market, measured by broad indexes such as the Standard & Poor's 500, tends to have a down year about once in every three. Thus, with an all-stock portfolio, the investor is taking about a one-in-three chance of having a net *loss* for a one-year period. With medium-term bonds (a popular debt investment) the chance of a down year is much smaller, about one year in ten.

Asset Allocation

Turn on "Wall Street Week" or virtually any other investment TV show and you'll likely see or hear some pundits opine about whether this is a good or bad time to buy stocks, or which are the good or bad stocks to buy. You hear this often enough and you might begin to believe it matters.

Actually, much of this information is trivia. Several years ago researchers examined the success of various investment portfolios and tracked the factors that accounted for different portfolios' results.* Here is what they found:

Asset Allocation	92%
Security Selection	3%
Market Timing	2%
Random (luck)	3%

Asset allocation, which is the decision to buy stocks, bonds, or some other investment, accounts for a whopping 92% of portfolio performance, yet you hardly hear about it on the investment shows.

* G. Brinson, L. R. Hood, and G. Beebower, "Determinants of Portfolio Performance," *Financial Analysts Journal,* July-August 1986; updated 1989.

It is, after all, fairly dry stuff, not like the who's-hot-who's-not analysis of individual stocks and markets. The actual stock picking and other security selection accounted for only 3% of performance, and market timing accounted for just 2%.

The great irony is that most people just seem to drift into the all-important decision on asset allocation. Whatever money happens to be available when the broker calls with a hot tip is what goes into stocks that day. A better approach is to look at your total portfolio, decide which classes of assets are over- or under-represented in light of your goals and risk tolerance, and only then consider a proposed investment.

For any given investment objective ("desired rate of return"), there is one theoretical asset allocation that provides the desired return at the minimum risk. This set of optimum portfolios makes up what analysts call the *efficient frontier.* Some money managers and do-it-yourself computer programs seek to recommend portfolios that come as close as possible to the efficient frontier, subject to some real-world constraints such as unwillingness to invest excessively in gold coins or real estate. Each investment advisor's version of the efficient frontier is unique, since each version depends on the assumptions the advisor is making for the risk and return of each asset class. But invariably, portfolios aiming for higher rewards/risk will allocate more assets to equities such as stocks, real estate, and commodities than do portfolios seeking income and stability of principal.

Unmarried couples have to decide whether they seek to have one overall asset allocation, or a separate one for each individual. Because of the potential problems in a breakup and the lack of a formal procedure comparable to divorce, I believe that except for couples in which the long-term commitment to each other is unquestioned and the estate planning is impeccable, the individual approach is much safer.

The Asset Allocation Worksheet set forth on the following pages will help you determine an appropriate arrangement for your own portfolio.

Asset Allocation Worksheet

NOTE: This worksheet helps you allocate your investments among stocks, bonds and money market instruments in a way that is consistent with your investment goals and tolerance for risk. Use this form in conjunction with the Goal-Setting Worksheet to develop an asset allocation that meets your financial needs without accepting undue risk.

Part 1: Compute Your Real Rate of Return for Various Investments

To complete this section you must estimate your future combined federal and state income tax rate. Based on historical performance (considering inflation), each investment category has a pretax rate of return listed in Column A. In Column B, enter 1 minus your estimated tax rate. (For example, if your estimated rate is 33%, you would enter 1−.33, or 67%.) Multiply the pretax return by your tax rate to find your estimated aftertax real rate of return for each investment, and enter the appropriate amounts in Column C.

	A	B	C
	Real Return Pretax	**Estimated Tax Rate**	**Real Return Aftertax**
Investment			
Treasury Bills	0.50%		
Bank Accounts, Money Market Funds	0.75%		
Long-Term Government Bonds	1.40%		
Long-Term Corporate Bonds	2.00%		
Common Stock	7.50%		

Asset Allocation Worksheet

Part 2: Define Your Risk Tolerance

Find the statement that best describes your willingness to accept investment risk.

Statement	Risk Tolerance
I seek maximum long-term growth of my capital. I do not care about receiving significant current payments of income, and I am willing to accept large fluctuations in the value of my investments.	Very High
I want significant long-term growth of my capital. However, I do not like extremely speculative investments and prefer to avoid excessive swings in portfolio value. Current income is a consideration, although secondary to achieving capital growth.	High
I want to achieve a balance between growth and income. Some portfolio swings, up to perhaps a 20% increase or decrease in total value over short periods, are acceptable; I am uncomfortable with larger swings. I am willing to sacrifice some long-term return to invest within these constraints.	Moderate
I want to achieve a reasonable rate of income from my portfolio. Capital growth is a secondary consideration, although it is nonetheless important to me. I do not wish to experience short-term fluctuations in portfolio value greater than about 15%.	Moderately Low
I want the value of my portfolio to be relatively stable. Slow but steady growth suits me, as long as I stay ahead of inflation. Income is an important secondary consideration; capital growth is not.	Low
I don't want to experience capital losses. I want my funds invested in only the most stable, secure places, and I do not wish to experience fluctuations in value greater than 5% to 10%. I am willing to experience periods when my real aftertax return (investment returns after taxes and inflation) are negative in order to achieve this safety.	Very Low

Asset Allocation Worksheet

Part 3: Suggested Portfolio Allocation

The table below suggests a sample portfolio allocation consisting of stocks, bonds, and money market funds for each risk tolerance identified in Part 2. Note that if you have significant short-term financial obligations and goals, investments in equities should be limited regardless of your risk tolerance.

	Suggested Allocation		
	Stocks	Bonds	Money Market
Risk Tolerance			
Very High	90%	5%	5%
High	80%	10%	10%
Moderate	50%	30%	20%
Moderately Low	30%	50%	20%
Low	15%	50%	35%
Very Low	10%	40%	50%

Part 4: Your Portfolio Allocation—Expected Real Rate of Return

NOTE: In this section you compute the anticipated real rate of return from the suggested portfolio allocation determined in Part 3.

	Stocks	Bonds	Money Market
Aftertax Real Return (from Part 1)			
x Portfolio Allocation (from Part 3)			
Aftertax Weighted Return			
	A	B	C

Add the aftertax weighted returns identified above (A, B, and C). This is your expected real rate of return from the suggested portfolio allocation.

You may find that this return is insufficient to finance the goals you have established elsewhere in this book. If so, you should reconsider your investment restrictions (that is, consider assuming more investment risk) or else scale down your financial objectives to a more realistic level.

Mutual Funds

The past fifteen years has brought phenomenal growth in the class
of investments known as mutual funds—companies that are set up
to let investors pool their resources and buy a basket of stocks,
bonds, or other assets in quantities much larger than the investors
could ever afford to acquire on their own.

Morningstar Mutual Funds, a newsletter that monitors the industry, counted more than four thousand funds operating in the United
States by the end of 1993. According to the Investment Company
Institute, a trade group, funds today hold more than $1.5 *trillion* in
assets. This is a tenfold increase in assets and a sixfold increase in
the number of funds since the beginning of the 1980s.

A mutual fund is a corporation. When you invest in it you are
technically buying shares in the corporation's stock. With most
funds (known as *open-end funds*) you do not sell these shares directly to other investors. Instead, you buy them from and sell them
to the fund itself at the "net asset value" of the fund. The net asset
value of most funds is determined daily and is printed in daily news-
papers near the stock market listings.

Mutual funds provide many advantages, including:

✓ **Diversification.** The typical fund holds dozens or
   hundreds of investments, usually spread across numerous
   companies and industries (unless the fund specifically
   seeks to concentrate on a certain type of investment,
   such as pharmaceutical companies).

✓ **Convenience.** Fund investments can be made by
   telephone or through automatic withdrawals from a
   savings or checking account. Earnings on your mutual
   fund investments can be sent to you in regular checks,
   automatically transferred to your bank account, or

automatically reinvested in the same or another mutual fund. Some funds allow you to get at your money by simply writing a check or *share draft,* for which part of your investment is automatically redeemed.

✓ **Easy changes of investment strategy.** Most large funds today are members of fund "families" that allow you to move your investments through a simple phone call (usually toll-free). You can sell your shares of a stock mutual fund and put the proceeds in a fund that invests in bonds, or *cash equivalents* (also known as *money market investments*).

✓ **Professional management.** Most people have neither the time, the skill, nor the inclination to study myriad companies in multiple industries to decide where to invest funds. Mutual funds are run by professional managers, who study companies in which they plan to invest and continue to review the investments once they are made.

✓ **Ease of acquisition and transfer.** This is a particular benefit for unmarried couples who want to share their investments with their partners. Usually you can open a mutual fund account as joint tenant with your domestic partner. In the event one of you dies, the other will automatically become the sole owner of the account regardless of the existence or provisions of any will.

Mutual funds have truly brought big-league investing within the reach of almost anyone. Most mutual fund accounts can be started with amounts ranging from about $1,500 to $3,000, and additional deposits can be made for as little as $50 or $100. Because the funds often trade tens of millions of dollars in securities at once, their shareholders benefit from razor-thin commissions and other economies of scale that very few individual investors could ever obtain.

Nothing this good comes free, however. The reason so many mutual funds exist is because their sponsors make money from them, a lot of money. Mutual funds investors may incur some or all of the following costs:

✓ **Sales charges, or loads.** Funds that are sold by brokers and other sales people usually charge an up-front fee that typically ranges from 3% to 5% but can be as high as 8.5%. On a fund with a 5% load, only 95 cents of the investor's dollar actually goes to work in his account. A smaller number of funds impose no sales charge on deposits, but charge a redemption fee or *back-end load* when you withdraw your money. In one sense this is slightly more fair, since if the fund manager has done a poor job and the value of your investment drops, so will the sales charge that you pay on the back end. On the other hand, this provision gives your broker a share of anything you make in the fund, since the commission on withdrawal will reflect any increase in the value of the shares you sell.

✓ **Management fees.** Funds usually pay their sponsors a management fee that may range from 0.2% to more than 1% of the fund's assets, billed annually. Funds also pay costs for record keeping, clerical assistance, and other operating expenses.

✓ **Sales and distribution fees, also known as 12-b (1) fees.** These are fees that are taken out of funds' assets (meaning the investors' pockets) to pay for the salespeople and other avenues by which the fund sponsor attracts more investors to the fund. Some funds that advertise themselves as "no-load" nonetheless take these kinds of fees.

Mutual funds are required to pay to their investors the fund's income from interest, dividends, and capital gains (the gain on investments that were sold) at least once per year. Most funds will give you an option to take your payments in cash or to have them reinvested automatically in additional shares of your fund.

The easy availability of mutual funds makes direct investment in stocks downright foolish for most people. Unless your portfolio is at least $500,000, and preferably $1 million, there is no way you can even approach the diversification and cost efficiency of a mutual fund; you probably also cannot justify the cost of hiring a good investment manager to assist you. You are also paying much higher commissions to your broker than a mutual fund would pay.

With so many existing mutual funds, how do you know which ones to invest in? Fortunately, a wealth of information is available. Virtually all financial publications do periodic or annual reviews of mutual fund investments; some of the most prominent are those published by *Money, Forbes, Fortune, Barron's,* and *Business Week. Morningstar Mutual Funds,* available at many libraries or directly from Morningstar in Chicago, is an excellent, concise service that covers more than 1,200 funds and ranks them on a one- to five-star rating scale. Dozens of specialized newsletters also cover the mutual fund industry, and there are numerous books on the subject.

Dollar-Cost Averaging

I mentioned earlier that the key to individual investing is self-discipline. Once you have determined your goals and selected an asset allocation and investment strategy to achieve them, you have to execute your plan consistently and with determination.

It sounds so easy, yet hardly anybody does this.

An asset allocation program will only work if you are committed to it and if you stick with it through thick and thin. Your time horizon has to be long enough to allow your program to work, as well. Five years is a minimum; ten years or more is better. (Retirement plans, since they are often in place for at least a few decades, are a *great* place to use an asset allocation program.)

Let me share a well-known but not well-used technique that will help you make your program work. The technique is called *dollar-cost averaging.* It works from the assumption, which has held up very well throughout this century, that stock prices trend steadily upward over long periods despite frequent short-term ups and downs.

Dollar-cost averaging requires you to make regular investments of a set amount of money at a fixed interval of time, such as $200 every month. When prices are low, your $200 will buy more shares; when prices are high, your $200 will buy fewer shares. Since prices over the long run will trend upward, you are doing what your grand-father might have taught you to do: Buy cheap, sell dear.

Now for one more trick to help your strategy work: *portfolio rebalancing.* Whenever investment prices change (such as when the stock market has had a big move up or down), you will probably find that your portfolio's asset allocation has drifted away from the original target. If stock prices have gone up, for example, stocks probably represent more of your investment assets than you had planned. You should periodically bring your asset allocation back into balance. Do this consistently and at regular intervals (once or twice a year); *don't* try to "time the market" by holding on to stocks until you believe they are about to go down. With dollar-cost aver-aging, you will automatically find yourself selling stocks when prices are high, and buying them when prices are low.

Putting It Together

Individually, many of the items discussed in this chapter may seem basic and even obvious; but that doesn't make the points less valid, especially since most people seem to honor them more in the breach than in the observance.

Here is a list of tips for putting together a successful investment strategy:

✓ **Know your goals.** If you don't know where you're going, you are not likely to get there.

✓ **Find an asset allocation that stands a good chance of achieving your goals, yet is not so risky that you are likely to abandon it along the way.** If you are investing jointly with your partner, make certain you both agree on the strategy and goals. Disagreement at the beginning can have all kinds of bad consequences down the road.

✓ **Unless you have at least $500,000, rely on mutual funds to give you diversification, low costs, and professional management.** If you are going to deviate from this policy, demand a good reason for doing so.

✓ **Give yourself twelve months to reach your desired asset allocation by first targeting where you put new investments, and second rearranging old investments in an orderly way.** Avoid making large, sudden sales and purchases, since this heightens the risk of moving at a bad time in the markets.

✓ **Make regular investments, at least every month.** Follow the adage to "pay yourself first." The best bet is to use automatic transfers from your bank account to your mutual fund to make investments. This practice avoids the risk that you'll forget, spend the money on something else first, or unwisely pay attention to someone on the radio who says he's certain the bottom is about to drop out of the market.

✓ **Rebalance your portfolio at least once a year, preferably every three to six months.** Pick a schedule and follow it religiously; don't succumb to temptation to let things ride because they have been going well so far. If you let anything drive itself far enough, it's going to crash and burn.

Good luck!

6

Parents and Children

At first the Census Bureau report seems astonishing: Nearly 1 million households in America headed by unmarried couples are home to children under age fifteen. Since many of those households have more than one child, we are talking about approximately 2 million kids.

On reflection, these figures are not so surprising. The increase in children living with unmarried parents is the result of at least three trends that have reshaped our society in the past thirty years. First, the rise in divorces has created many single parents with sole custody of their children. Simultaneously, we have seen a sharp increase in births to unwed mothers, who range from teenage girls to highly paid careerwomen. And, finally, broader acceptance of unmarried cohabitation made it more likely that these parents would set up housekeeping with another adult without getting married. (To see these trends, look at television. One era gave us "The Brady Bunch" while another produced "Who's the Boss?")

Parental Rights and Obligations

Our laws recognize that parents have a right (and a duty) to direct the upbringing of their children, subject only to broad community standards of acceptable care, discipline, and education. At the same time, parents are obligated to provide financial support consistent with their means. In most states children are seen as having claims equal or superior to the rights of the parent's spouse. This status is reflected, for example, in the laws governing intestacy. Children whose married parent dies without a will are typically entitled to at least half, and sometimes more, of the deceased parent's property.

Of course, there is often a chasm between theory and practice; witness the huge numbers of parents who somehow avoid making court-ordered child-support payments. It is also not unusual to have the parental rights of an individual terminated, either voluntarily, such as by placing a child for adoption, or involuntarily, by the legal removal of the child from the home.

Although all states impose a burden on parents to support their children, the definition of *support* varies from state to state and even from parent to parent. Is a parent obliged to pay for summer camp? Private tutors? College tuition? Medical school? Support depends on the circumstances.

In theory, the marital status of the parent does not affect these support obligations. In paternity suits, courts have long imposed support payments on unwed fathers. Today the law is only beginning to evolve to cope with the roles of surrogate mothers, sperm and egg donors, and birth parents who change their minds about (or, in the case of fathers, are unaware of) adoptions.

Paying Up

Suppose a child is born to married parents who later divorce. At least three significant financial issues will be addressed in the divorce proceeding. They are the *property settlement, alimony,* and *child support.*

Property settlements and alimony represent amounts that one divorcing spouse will retain or receive from the other. In common-law states, *property settlements* will usually award premarital and other separate property to its owner while providing an equitable (which may not mean equal!) distribution to each spouse of property accumulated during the marriage. In community-property states, the separate property goes to each spouse while community property is automatically deemed to be owned 50% by each.

Alimony is a stipend that one spouse (historically the woman) receives from the other for her own support. The original justification probably was that upon marriage the husband made a promise to provide lifetime support to his wife, and thus he should not be relieved of this burden when he later divorced his wife. More recently alimony has been seen as an interim measure to provide support while a woman is still preoccupied with child rearing, or while she completes or updates her education, or while she reestablishes her value in the job market. Alimony these days is also sometimes awarded to males, for the same reasons.

Child support, on the other hand, is what the divorcing parent owes his or her *children* as their birthright. The child's living standard should not suffer unduly merely because the parents choose to live apart. Therefore, a child who could have expected private schools and country clubs if the parents had stayed married is likely to draw more child support than the offspring who could expect public schools and parks.

The table below compares these three types of payments.

A great deal of divorce negotiation (and litigation) centers

	Property Settlement	Alimony	Child Support
One-Time or Periodic	One time (may be payable in installments)	Periodic	Periodic
Recipient	Ex-spouse	Ex-spouse	Ex-spouse for benefit of children
Duration	Obligation terminates when property is divided and transferred	Until death of either spouse, remarriage of recipient, or earlier date as ordered by court	Until child completes education, reaches legal adulthood, or as ordered by court
Taxation	Transfers between spouses incident to divorce are not taxed	Generally, deductible by payer and taxable income to recipient	Not deductible by payer, not taxable income to recipient

around the amount and nature of payments that will be made between spouses. The spouse who will be doing the paying has an obvious incentive to characterize payments as alimony, since that will give the payer a tax deduction while creating taxable income for the recipient. When the payer is in a higher tax bracket than the recipient, this can create a net gain that can then be shared between the parties. (To avoid letting people take advantage of this, Congress has enacted *front-loading* rules that prevent property settlements from being disguised as alimony.)

However, in most cases, the receiving spouse will want an obligation characterized as property settlement or child support. This classification can be critical if the receiving spouse later remarries, since alimony will almost always terminate upon remarriage while a child-support obligation usually continues. There are doubtless many couples who would get married except for the fact that one member would have to forego alimony payments. It is not unusual to see alimony agreements that terminate if the receiving spouse "lives as husband and wife" with another individual outside marriage.

If you are a divorced parent and receive alimony or child support, it is very important to understand the conditions in which it might terminate. Depending upon how your agreement or court order is written, you might lose substantial income simply by taking a domestic partner. If you later receive gifts from your partner, you might also undercut your right to receive alimony or your child's right to receive support. In this case, you will need to plan carefully any property-sharing arrangement you might reach with your new domestic partner. We discussed these types of arrangements in Chapter Two.

Guardians, Custodians, and Trustees

Most parents want to provide for the financial welfare of their children. As we have seen earlier, this generally requires the appointment of an adult to safeguard the children themselves as well as their property. In this section we look at the various roles the adult might play.

The biggest role is, of course, that of the parent. If you are an unmarried domestic partner with a child, the best way to ensure that your partner continues to live with and care for your child following your death or disability is to have your partner adopt the child. Sometimes this is not possible, such as when the child's other natural parent is alive and retains parental rights, or if you and your partner are homosexual in a jurisdiction that prohibits or raises obstacles to adoptions by gays and Lesbians. But sometimes an adoption can be arranged following the termination of the other natural parent's legal rights and obligations toward the child. The following case will illustrate.

♣ CASE 1: The White Knight

George was an alcoholic, abusive husband and father. Beverly married him when she was nineteen to escape a troubled home life. Two children, Danny and Dolly, were born within three years. As time passed, George's drinking worsened, and his temper took a nasty turn when he lost his job and could not get steady work. Finally, when Danny and Dolly were twelve and ten, Beverly moved out.

She took a job as a receptionist and won a court order requiring George to pay $600 a month in child support. He made one payment, stopped for a year, made a couple of other sporadic payments, and finally dropped out of sight. Beverly took a second job at night to make ends meet, relying on her mother to look after the children.

Three years later Beverly's company hired a new senior vice president for marketing. Arthur, a widower, was kind and sympathetic, and soon began taking Beverly and the kids for weekend trips to art shows, theme parks, and boat races. Beverly quit her jobs, went back to school, and moved into Arthur's home with her children. She also asked the court to terminate George's parental rights. After two years she won, and Arthur legally adopted the children.

While suing to terminate George's parental rights Beverly discovered she had an inoperable form of uterine cancer. She died a month after Arthur's adoption of the children became final. George then went back to court seeking to reinstate his rights and regain custody of the children, but a judge dismissed his case for failing to state any grounds upon which Arthur's parental status could be revoked.

The next closest role that an adult can play under the law to a minor is that of *guardian.* A guardian usually has custody of the children and is responsible for their physical and emotional welfare. As we have seen in Chapter Three, you should nominate a guardian for your minor children in your will. It is not a bad idea to nominate also a guardian in a separate letter that could be brought before a judge in the event you are incapacitated but remain alive, a situation in which your will does not apply.

Courts will ordinarily award custody of a child to the surviving biological parent unless that person's parental rights have been terminated or the parent is demonstrably unfit for the job. "Demonstrably unfit" is a matter of opinion. Many divorced parents consider their ex-spouse demonstrably unfit for practically everything, most of all raising children, but a judge might not agree. If you are going to nominate someone other than a surviving parent as guardian of your child, make the strongest possible argument in your will or a separate testamentary letter.

Gay couples face special problems in this area because some judges may simply refuse to grant custody to a homosexual. In one widely publicized but rather aberrant case, a Virginia judge even deprived a surviving natural mother of custody and assigned a child to his grandmother, simply because the child's mother was a lesbian. On the other hand, the general trend in the courts has been to allow homosexuals to exercise parental or guardianship rights. If you want your gay partner to share responsibility for your child, the best answer may be to start adoption proceedings while you are alive.

A *custodian* is an adult who, legally, maintains custody of property that actually belongs to the child. Most people are familiar with custodial arrangements in connection with bank accounts. An account may belong to a child and be taxable in his or her name, but until the child reaches majority an adult has the right to control deposits and withdrawals. The custodial relationship is usually created by signing some papers when bank accounts and similar relationships are established.

A *trustee* is in a similar but more formal relationship. The trustee is the person who becomes legal owner of property that is placed in a trust. The trust is managed for the benefit of the beneficiaries, who may be entitled to receive the trust property at some point in the future. Modern trusts are almost always in writing and are often established for tax and other estate-planning reasons.

Transferring Property to Children

Parents give money to children for many reasons. Children may also accumulate significant amounts of money from other relatives' gifts and inheritances, or from earnings ranging from newspaper routes to acting and modeling fees.

Money that children themselves earn is, of course, their own. Many states have established strict rules over when and how parents may gain control over such funds. Parental control is often the best option in caring for funds a child earns, however, because a child who may be able to earn a big income is not necessarily mature enough to know what to do with it. But there have been numerous abuses in the past, most obviously in certain show-business families, so courts and legislatures have cracked down.

Property that children acquire from others is usually governed under the Uniform Transfers to Minors Act (UTMA) or its predecessor, the Uniform Gifts to Minors Act (UGMA). All states have adopted one or the other of these laws, although in some cases with modifications.

The UGMA generally covers gifts of money, securities, life insurance, and annuities. A custodian is designated to control the property for the minor's exclusive benefit until legal majority, generally ages eighteen or twenty-one, at which time the property goes outright to the child. The UTMA works in much the same way, but it allows other types of property (real estate, for example) to be transferred to the child.

These uniform laws make transfers to children simple and inexpensive, but they do not work well in every situation. One obvious case: A parent who provides a large inheritance or life insurance benefit for a child might not want the total sum to go outright to the child at the relatively young age of majority. Instead, the parent might want to have a more mature individual retain control and perhaps pass the property to the child in stages at ages twenty-five, thirty, or later. For these situations, trusts are a better choice.

Should you be the custodian of your child's UGMA/UTMA account? If you are the source of the funds (i.e., the account will receive gifts from you to the child) the conventional wisdom is no, because of potential tax complications. Taxes will generally be a problem only if your federal gross estate is more than $600,000, or if you use funds from the account to pay expenses for the child that are legally part of *your* obligation to provide support. For most people in most situations, however, the parent can serve as custodian with little risk of harm.

What about having your domestic partner serve as custodian? This option has several advantages. It avoids the potential estate-tax problem you would have if you fill the role yourself; it strengthens the relationship between your partner and the child (and can be brought to the attention of a judge who may be deciding guardianship), and, if anything happens to you, your domestic partner presumably will still be around. On the other hand, you should be very confident in your partner's integrity and in the strength of your relationship. Legally, your partner cannot invade the custodial account for his or her own benefit, but that will be little comfort if your partner flees to Tahiti with your child's college fund. Likewise, if you and your partner go separate ways, you won't find a continued financial relationship appealing, and changing custodians may be inconvenient.

Children's Net Worth Statement

Date:

Child:

	Current Value	Tax Cost (A)	Potential Tax on Sale (B)	Net Value
Bank Accounts				
Money Market Funds				
Bonds				
Stocks				
Other Assets				
Less: Loans	( )		( )	( )
Net Worth				

Child:

	Current Value	Tax Cost (A)	Potential Tax on Sale (B)	Net Value
Bank Accounts				
Money Market Funds				
Bonds				
Stocks				
Other Assets				
Less: Loans	( )		( )	( )
Net Worth				

Child:

	Current Value	Tax Cost (A)	Potential Tax on Sale (B)	Net Value
Bank Accounts				
Money Market Funds				
Bonds				
Stocks				
Other Assets				
Less: Loans	( )		( )	( )
Net Worth				

NOTES:

(A) Tax cost, or basis, is the amount invested in the asset for tax purposes. The greater the basis, the less the potential tax when the asset is sold.

(B) Potential tax on sale is the estimated tax due if the asset were sold immediately. Generally, investments that have been held more that one year are taxed at preferential capital gains rates.

Ready for Retirement

Married couples almost always assume that their financial futures are linked, and they make their plans accordingly. The law protects them by providing surviving spouses with automatic pension and Social Security benefits.

Unmarried couples may or may not plan to be together down the road at retirement, and people who live together after retirement may be unsure about whether the arrangement will last the rest of their days. And the law provides no automatic protection: Unmarried partners have no rights to each other's pensions or Social Security benefits. Sometimes it is possible for a surviving heterosexual partner to gain survivor benefits by proving in court that the relationship was in fact a common-law marriage. (In one case, a New York court recognized common-law marriage because the couple had visited relatives in a common-law marriage jurisdiction together two or three times a year.) However, by far the safest approach is to make retirement plans for each individual rather than for the couple as a unit.

The bottom line for domestic partners is that without careful planning, one or both may end up without the cash cushion that makes for a comfortable retirement.

How Much Is Enough?

A white male born in this country in 1890 could expect to live 42.5 years; a white female, 44.5. A century later those figures had climbed to 72.7 and 79.2 years, respectively. More importantly, an individual who reached age 60 a century ago had, on average, about 15 more years to live; today the figure is closer to 21 years.

Most people's primary financial concern is to make certain that their money does not expire before they do. The problem is that while we can tell *on average* how long an individual of a certain age is likely to live, we usually have no idea *for a specific individual* whether the life span after retirement will be brief or lengthy. We therefore have two choices: We can create financial structures that work on the basis of predictable averages, or we can make individual arrangements and take a risk by betting on our life expectancy.

As we shall see, the retirement funding system in this country uses both approaches to some extent.

The following table compares the various major sources of retirement funding.

The table* shows how different combinations of retirement funding sources can produce a variety of desirable results, such as survivor protection and an inflation hedge. A well-designed retirement financial plan tries to strike the right balance among the factors we will now consider.

Steady income. A desirable feature of a retirement funding source is the built-in ability to disburse a predictable amount of money at regular intervals. Employment meets this need, of course, since a regular paycheck fits the description of steady income. Interest and dividends from conservative, income-oriented investments

---

* Although municipal bonds and other tax-free investments are available, some of the benefit is lost through lower investment returns.

	Wages	Investments	Social Security	Pension (Def. Ben.)	Pension (Def. Cont.)	Life Insurance	Annuity
Steady Income	Yes	Possible	Yes	Yes	Possible	No	Yes
COLA?	Possible	Possible	Yes	Seldom	Possible	Possible	Seldom
Lasts Lifetime?	No	No	Yes	Yes	No	No	Yes
Taxable?	Yes	Yes*	Maybe	Yes	Yes	No	Yes
Helps Survivors?	No	Yes	Yes	Possible	Yes	Yes	Possible

* Although municipal bonds and other tax-free investments are available, some of the benefit is lost through lower investment returns.

also qualify. Defined benefit pension plans and Social Security also fit the bill, as do commercial annuities sold mainly by insurance companies. (In an annuity, you make either one or a series of payments up front, the "accumulation phase," and after investing the funds for a certain period of time, the insurance company begins making regular payments to you or, in some cases, your designated beneficiaries, the "distribution phase.")

Cost of living adjustment (COLA). Inflation is the archenemy of retirees, whose income is largely fixed. Inflation has received relatively little attention in recent years as it declined from double-digit levels during the 1970s to below 4% through much of the 1980s and early '90s. But even modest amounts of inflation can do great harm over the span of a retirement. The graph below shows how the value of a dollar declines over a period of thirty years at 4% annual inflation. Over the thirty-year period inflation reduces the dollar's purchasing power to only about 31 cents, *with nearly half of the decline occurring within the first ten years.* Obviously, if we should see a return to the higher inflation rates of several decades ago, the impact on retirees would be even more severe. To see exactly how severe, turn to the Inflation Matrix in the Appendix.

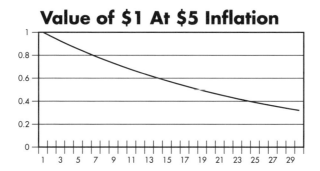

Value of $1 At $5 Inflation

Lasts for lifetime. Several of the retirement funding vehicles shown in the table address the risk that you will live "too long" by, in effect, spreading the risk among large numbers of people. Social

Security is the best example. The benefits are guaranteed for life and are an obligation of the U.S. government. If you buy an annuity from an insurance company you get the same deal, except that the guarantee is no stronger than the financial strength of the company that makes it. Defined-benefit pensions also promise a lifetime pay-out, backed by the financial strength of your employer's pension fund and the federal Pension Benefit Guaranty Corporation. Of course, the down side of these lifetime-oriented funding sources is that you might work a lifetime to earn them, only to die shortly after beginning to collect. This usually means your family gets little or no benefit, although there are some exceptions. (We discuss the exceptions under "Benefits for Survivors" below.)

Taxable or tax-free investments. Everyone hates to pay taxes, and often retirees (or people approaching retirement) are tempted to seek out tax-free sources of income. What may seem to be logical is really upside-down thinking. Often retirees are in low enough tax brackets that they would be better off seeking higher-yield taxable income sources rather than lower-yield tax exempts.

Wages and self-employment income are always taxable, of course, except when earned in very small amounts. Retirees who are receiving Social Security face an extra burden because their benefits may be reduced if they earn too much money, and also because Social Security benefits are themselves partially subject to tax once income reaches certain levels.

Most pension and profit-sharing plans are *tax deferred,* meaning you do not pay tax on interest, dividends, and capital gains earned in your retirement account until you begin withdrawing the money, which can be decades later. This tax deferral is very valuable, as it allows you to compound the growth of your initial investment. Most commercial annuities have a similar tax-deferred feature.

Life insurance is tax-deferred if you withdraw the cash value while you are alive. A life insurance death benefit paid to your survivor is usually *tax-free.*

Benefits for survivors. Generally, the investments that do not provide lifetime protection are the richest sources of cash for survivors if you die prematurely. A generous investment fund that was to carry you through twenty years of touring the world will not have been spent if you die in a car crash on the way to the airport for your first trip. Your untimely death will, at least, mean a windfall of sorts for your survivors. The same applies to defined-contribution pension and profit-sharing plans. Life insurance policies by their nature are more beneficial to survivors than to the owner. However, if your survivors rely on a policy on *your* life, they will be at risk of outliving the insurance money unless they use it to buy a commercial annuity. If you buy an annuity for your own benefit, you will have a choice of whether to provide survivor protection.

Preretirement Planning

Building that tidy nest egg has to start long before retirement. Let's look at some strategies for accumulating those funds.

Retirement plans and surrogates. The unmarried couple does not receive automatic survivor benefits in most employer-sponsored retirement plans. In many cases, however, a retiring employee can elect a joint-and-survivor benefit that covers a non-spouse. An employee who is too young to retire could either name his (or her) domestic partner to receive any vested benefits (such designation is revocable in case you later break up), or could have the benefit made payable to his estate and grant the domestic partner rights to the funds under his will. It is generally better to designate your domestic partner, rather than your estate, as beneficiary of the retirement plan. If you die before benefit payments commence, your named beneficiary can receive payments over his or her full life expectancy, while your estate would be required to take the money by the end of the fifth full calendar year after your death. Once the money is distributed to your estate, the benefit of tax deferral is lost.

Life insurance. If your domestic partner's income is going to die with him or her, and you count on that income for your own needs, what can you do? Well, you can pay someone else to take on the risk of your mate's premature death. Life insurance does this for you. Insurance and annuity products also can be used to accumulate cash to supplement retirement plans, which is why many companies provide insurance-oriented supplemental benefit plans to their top executives. Chapter Eleven provides a detailed discussion of life insurance products.

Individual Retirement Accounts. The law gives a significant advantage to unmarried couples who have only one member covered by a tax-favored (also known as *qualified*) retirement plan at work. In this situation, the other member of the couple is still able to contribute up to $2,000 (or his entire earned income, if less) to a deductible IRA. In the case of married couples, coverage by one spouse in a qualified plan reduces or precludes deductible IRA contributions by either spouse if their combined incomes are above $40,000.

The following case illustrates this situation.

▲ CASE 1: Salting It Away

Adam and Fred have been lovers for five years and expect to remain together for the rest of their lives. Both are forty years old. Fred, a computer management specialist, works for a large corporation that maintains a profit-sharing plan. Fred puts $5,000 per year into the plan and the company contributes a matching $2,500. Adam is manager of a small bookstore in the suburban village where they live. His employer does not maintain any kind of retirement plan.

Recently Adam's new accountant suggested that he contribute $2,000 per year to a deductible IRA. At Adam's 28% tax bracket he will save $560 in taxes, making the out-of-pocket cost of contributing just $1,440. If the IRA grows at 9% per year and Adam continues making $2,000 annual contributions, he will accumulate $184,648 by age sixty-five (but he will owe taxes on that money when he withdraws it). Fred hopes to achieve the same 9% growth in his profit-sharing account; if he does, assuming $7,500 total annual contributions, he will amass $692,430.

If Adam and Fred were married, Adam would not be eligible to make deductible IRA contributions because their combined income is more than $40,000. However, he could make *nonde-ductible* contributions and accumulate the same $184,648. The out-of-pocket cost will be higher because of the lack of tax benefits, but at withdrawal Adam will not have to pay tax on the $50,000 he contributed, making the taxable portion of his IRA only $134,648.

Other Investments

If retirement is still many years in the future, growth-oriented investments are the way to go. Many people in their thirties and forties are much too conservative in their retirement savings portfolios, investing in bonds, money market accounts, and insurance company debt ("guaranteed investment contracts" or GICs) that historically perform only about half as well as equities. The key, as we discussed in Chapter Five, is to be diversified and to have an asset allocation strategy that limits the ups and downs of your portfolio to a level you can handle so that you stick with your program.

Another investment possibility is real estate. It can be bought through a close cousin of mutual funds, the Real Estate Investment Trust (REIT), or you might buy individual properties. The latter approach is undiversified and therefore much riskier. On the other hand, the price of attractive retirement properties may rise sharply when the Baby Boom generation starts to retire. If you find a place today to which you might be interested in retiring, buying early might not be a bad idea if you can afford it.

Planning at Retirement

Eventually, retirement day rolls around and we take inventory of what we have. The essential question now is: What kind of lifestyle can I afford?

Unfortunately, but not surprisingly, there is no simple or single answer. How much you can afford depends on what kind of assumptions you make about your future (and how accurate your assumptions turn out to be). Implicitly or explicitly, in setting your budget in retirement you will be making assumptions about:

✓ future inflation

✓ future tax rates

✓ the performance of your investments

✓ your life span

If you change any one of these variables, the lifestyle you can afford changes, also. The best you can do is make an educated guess and then take stock periodically so that you can make adjustments as required.

Let's start by looking at future inflation and future tax rates. We have already seen how inflation will erode the value of a dollar. When it comes to your investments, tax rates will also take a bite since taxes reduce the amount of interest, dividends, and capital gains that you are able to keep and reinvest.

For example, Waldo invests $10,000 for a 10% rate of return. He is in the 30% tax bracket and inflation is 3%. Here is what happens after one year:

Initial investment	$10,000
Interest income	1,000
	$11,000
Lost buying power	
(3% of $10,000)	(300)
Tax on $1,000 interest	(300)
Investment at end of year	$10,400

Waldo's 10% *nominal rate of return* translated to a 4% *real rate of return* once taxes and inflation were considered. This is the formula:

Real Return = Nominal Return – Tax Rate – Inflation Rate

For individuals in the top tax brackets, the historic experience has been that very conservative investments (Treasury bills and money market funds, for example) have had real rates of return from about 0 to –2%; portfolios that are balanced between equities, bonds, and cash range from 0 to +2%; mixed stock and bond portfolios run from +1% to +3%; and growth-oriented portfolios can expect rates of +3% to +5%. If you know the type of investments you favor and your tax bracket, you can make an educated guess at your real rate of return.

Note that we do not require you to guess at future inflation, even though it is an important variable. There is a reason for this. We are assuming that the relationship between investment performance and inflation is relatively stable; that is, in times of low inflation, investment yields will be lower and in times of high inflation they will be higher, so that a particular type of investment will have the same *real* rate of return regardless of inflation. Over long periods of time this has generally been true, although in shorter periods, such as the high-inflation 1970s, some real returns dropped markedly.

Now, make an estimate of your portfolio's real rate of return. If you expect to keep a balance of stocks and bonds, for example, a +2% estimate is not unreasonable. The next question is: How long will your portfolio last if you make withdrawals equal to X dollars (not counting future inflation; your actual withdrawals will rise as spending power declines). Let's use a hypothetical case as an example.

⚓ CASE 2: Setting the Retirement Budget

Minnie had accumulated $200,000 in retirement savings. As retirement approached, she calculated that she would want to spend $10,000 annually out of that retirement fund, above what she would receive and spend from Social Security and her employer's pension. Minnie figured that her *capital-to-expense ratio* was 20—that is, she had $20 on hand for each $1 of annual spending that she wanted to do in retirement. She also assumed that she would earn a real rate of return of +2% on her $200,000 while it was invested.

At a financial planning seminar Minnie received a Capital Sufficiency Table, like the one in the Appendix of this book. She used the table to finish her calculation. She looked down the leftmost column to find the line for a capital-to-expense ratio of 20. Then she moved across the columns to the right until she reached the one for a real rate of return of +2%. There she found the figure "27.8." The table was telling her that at a real rate of return of +2% and a capital-to-expense ratio of 20, her retirement fund would be exhausted in 27.8 years. Since Minnie was already sixty-five, she relaxed; by the time the money was exhausted she either would not be alive or would be in her nineties, with a slower lifestyle that could be maintained by Social Security and her employer's pension.

Careful budgeting is one of the keys to a financially successful retirement. We have very little control over inflation and taxes, and only moderate control over investment performance. We have much more control over spending, however. The next case illustrates.

⏺ CASE 3: Tightening the Belt

Daisy was best friends with Minnie, whom we met in Case 2. Daisy, like Minnie, was sixty-five and contemplating retirement, and she also expected to achieve a real return on her investments of +2%. She also had the same $200,000 investment portfolio. But while Minnie felt she only needed to spend $10,000 a year of that money, Daisy felt she needed to spend $20,000. Her capital-to-expense ratio therefore was 10 ($200,000 divided by $20,000).

Daisy did not attend the financial planning seminar with Minnie, but Minnie showed her the capital sufficiency table and how to use it. Daisy was shocked to find that at a capital-to-expense ratio of 10 and a +2% real return her money would be gone in just 12.2 years. She planned to live longer than that! She wanted her money to last at least 20 years, so she moved her finger up the +2% column until she found the entries 19.4 (for a capital-to-expense ratio of 16) and 21.0 (for a capital-to-expense ratio of 17). A 20-year duration would require a capital-to-expense ratio somewhere between them, or around 16.5, she figured.

Daisy realized she had two choices. She could try to scrape up enough capital to equal 16.5 times her annual spending of

$20,000, but that would mean building her investment fund from $200,000 to $330,000. There was no way to do that! The only other choice was to cut her budget. She divided $200,000 by 16.5 and got $12,121. If she held her budget to that level, her capital-to-expense ratio would be 16.5 and her money would last the required 20 years. Daisy began looking for places to cut back.

Daisy's case demonstrates the power of *leverage*. If the desired capital-to-expense ratio is, say, 20, then every $1 cut from your annual spending reduces the required investment fund by $20. It will usually be much easier to cut spending than to find so much additional investment capital.

I have provided a Retirement Budget worksheet on the following page to help you plan your own retirement spending.

Retirement Budget

This worksheet will help you estimate, in future dollars, the income and expenses you can expect to experience when you retire. Any shortfall (excess of expenses over income) will have to be made up from your investments. You can use the information developed here in conjunction with the Capital Sufficiency Table and the Financial Goals Worksheet (see Appendix) to determine whether your anticipated retirement portfolio is adequate to support your planned spending.

To project future amounts you will need either a financial calculator or an ordinary hand-held calculator together with a table of future values of $1. (You can use the college funding Matrix; see Appendix.) This worksheet allows you to specify a separate rate of increase for each item, since some prices (such as health care) have historically increased at rates different from the general rate of inflation.

Number of Years to Retirement:

Income	Current Year	Rate of Increase	Estimate at Retirement
Your Earnings		n/a	
Your Pension		n/a	
Domestic Partner Earnings (Opt.)		n/a	
Domestic Partner Pension (Opt.)		n/a	
Your Social Security		n/a	
Domestic Partner Social Security (Opt.)		n/a	
Other			
Other			
Total Income			

Expenses			
Fixed Expenses			
Taxes & Withholding			
Groceries			
Mortgage			
Other Loans & Credit Crads			
Property Tax			
Utilities			
Home Maintenance			
Clothing & Dry Cleaning			
Uninsured Medical & Dental			
Child Care			
Car Loans			
Gasoline & Oil			
Car Repairs & Maintenance			
Insurance: Life, Home, Car			
Tuition			
Total Fixed Expenses			
Variable Expenses			
Major Purchases			
Restaurants			
Entertainment			
Telephone			
Vacation			
Books, CDs, Magazines			
Fitness			
Personal Grooming			
Gifts			
Charitable Donations			
Other			
Total Variable Expenses			
Total Expenses			
SURPLUS OR SHORT FALL			

Social Security

For over half a century Social Security has been the cornerstone of the American retirement funding system. Yet despite its age and importance, there is a great deal of confusion about how Social Security works.

The Roosevelt administration had several goals when it proposed Social Security in the 1930s. Providing a basic level of support for the elderly was an important objective, but another major goal, in the midst of the Depression, was to induce older workers to retire so that younger workers could more easily get jobs. The plan was to impose a payroll tax on workers and their employers to finance a set of basic retirement, disability, and survivor's benefits.

Of course there were some Americans who really did not need government benefits, even during the Depression. Providing benefits to them would make the entire program more costly. Yet it was politically impractical to turn Social Security into a "welfare" program. Instead, it was advertised as a plan in which everyone "paid for his own benefits" through contributions to a "trust fund." But as the system evolved, the plan changed. Social Security has become a system that transfers money from today's workers to yesterday's workers.

In recent decades the program has expanded dramatically. Medicare was created in 1965 to provide basic medical benefits to retirees. In the 1970s Congress ruled that benefits would rise in conjunction with inflation. This measure greatly increased the cost of the system, so that in the early 1980s a substantial increase in the Social Security (FICA) tax was needed. Also at that time, the law was changed to gradually increase the normal retirement age above sixty-five (which it had been since Social Security's creation). For individuals who reach sixty-five after the year 1999, normal retirement will be delayed by two months per year until the year 2022, which will ultimately raise the retirement age to sixty-seven for individuals born in 1960 or later.

In 1991 and 1993, rising medical costs forced increases in the Medicare portion of the Social Security tax. Today the Social Security system does take in a bit more than it spends, but this excess is used to offset part of the enormous budget deficit the Treasury incurs in other areas.

Social Security benefits are not lavish by today's standards, but they still play an important role in many people's finances. The maximum benefit for an individual retiring at age sixty-five in 1993 was about $1,128 per month, or $13,536 per year; this top benefit would generally go to individuals who made at least $57,600 before retirement. In addition, a spouse of this individual would be entitled to an additional $564 per month even if the spouse had never worked, and the spouse could get a higher amount if his or her own earnings record supported it.

Social Security does not extend any benefits to unmarried domestic partners. Not only is there no spousal retirement benefit, there is no survivor death benefit and no disability protection.

Medicare and ''Medigap''

In 1965, Congress added Medicare to the Social Security program. Medicare provides hospital and major-medical coverage to individuals age sixty-five or older, as well as to younger individuals who are disabled.

Medicare's hospital coverage is automatically extended to anyone sixty-five or older collecting Social Security retirement benefits. If you are still working past age sixty-five you must apply to be covered under Medicare hospital benefits; you should do this about three months before your sixty-fifth birthday. Hospital coverage is also extended automatically to anyone who has been collecting Social Security disability payments for at least twenty-four months. An important addition to the program came in 1990, when former disability recipients who have returned to work were allowed to buy Medicare hospital coverage. These people often have difficulty obtaining private insurance because of their recent disability.

Medical coverage (also known as Medicare "Part B"), which pays for non-hospital doctor care and other services, requires payment of a separate monthly premium.

Medicare does not provide good coverage for long-term illness, and it provides no coverage at all for "custodial care," such as nursing homes for people who are not acutely ill but can no longer care for themselves.

The gaps for long-term illness are filled by "medigap" policies offered by private insurance companies. Just a few years ago there were hundreds of such policies on the market, offering coverage so confusing that many people bought three or four policies in self-defense. This sorry situation ended in 1992, when new legislation required all policies to fit one of ten designs labeled *A* for the most basic, through *J* for the most comprehensive. Not all companies will offer all categories, but one company's *A* coverage, *B* coverage, et cetera, will be just like another's, except for the price. Now you can shop around for the best deal.

Medigap does not, however, cover custodial care. Yet another variety of private insurance, known as *long-term care,* or LTC policies, is sold for that need. Otherwise, individuals rely on their own assets or on Medicaid, the state-federal medical program for the poor.

Medicaid
A thorough discussion of Medicaid and its use in nursing home and other custodial-care settings could require a whole book. We will simply note a few general points, the most important of which is that this is another case in which not being married to your domestic partner can be a distinct advantage (if you plan carefully).

Medicaid rules require applicants to spend nearly all their assets before the government will begin paying for nursing home and other medical care. An individual's home is generally exempt from this requirement if he or she plans to return to it after discharge from the nursing home. A minimal amount of other assets is also exempt, and spouses are allowed to keep a larger exempt amount. Medicaid also has strict income limits. If a recipient exceeds the income guidelines, he or she has to turn the excess over to the state to reimburse the costs Medicaid has covered. The actual figures vary from state to state, and there are many technical requirements. You can get more information from local social service offices, senior citizens groups, and lawyers and accountants who specialize in issues affecting the elderly.

Giving away your assets is of limited value due to the thirty-six-month *look-back* rule: Any asset you give away in the thirty-six months prior to applying for Medicaid is treated, for purposes of eligibility, as if you still owned it. (This look-back period extends to sixty months for assets you give to a trust. Prior law required only a thirty-month look-back for both outright and trust gifts, but was changed by the 1993 federal budget and tax law.)

Conventional Medicaid planning generally has people give away all but the assets they will need to pay for nursing home and other expenses in the coming thirty-six months. This way, at least any assets beyond those needed for the thirty-six-month period are spared from the spend-down rules. Once the look-back period has passed, Medicaid benefits can be obtained.

The advantage of being an unmarried couple is clear. Any property owned by the non-spouse partner will not be counted in the Medicaid eligibility calculation, as long as it was not received as a gift from the other partner in the thirty-six-month look-back period. For couples in which one member is significantly older or frailer than the other, concentrating assets in the hands of the stronger partner can be a way around the Medicaid rules. Of course, the same warning applies here as in other situations where property is transferred: You have to be sure of your relationship with your partner.

8

When You Own the Business

Most people, no matter how much they love their mates, are probably at least a little relieved to have a workplace that is separate from their home life. It is one thing to adjust to your lover's quirks; it is quite another to put up with them twenty-four hours a day.

But there are those couples who choose to work as well as live together, and often they seem to thrive on it. These people have truly entered a partnership in which their lives as well as their livelihoods are linked. We are not talking here about people who soldier together in the corporate trenches; they at least have the structure of a large organization to provide some variety and insulation. This chapter is dedicated to the hard-core joint venturers, the couple who chooses to operate a business together. In this chapter, we will assume that you have taken the plunge and joined your domestic partner in the workplace.

Who's in Charge?

There are two basic scenarios in working with your mate. One of you works *for* the other, or you work *with* each other. Neither is necessarily better, but things are liable to get messy unless you know which applies to you.

Sometimes it's an easy call. If one of you is a licensed dentist and the other is answering the phones, don't fool yourself into thinking that you have a 50-50 arrangement. Even if you both wanted it to be that way, it couldn't; the person with professional responsibility has got to call the shots.

Usually the situation will be much less clear. You may have both had similar training and backgrounds, or perhaps you have very different skills such as production and accounting. I have seen too many businesses in which "shared responsibility" really means "we want to avoid a fight about who is in charge."

Don't give in to this kind of buck-passing. If you are both trying to make a living from the same enterprise, you have twice the incentive to make certain it succeeds. Success is much more likely when there are clear expectations, concrete goals, and accountability for achieving them.

If the two of you are going to be in business together, sit down and explicitly agree to a relationship along one of the following lines:

✓ **You are partners working together.** You are each responsible for the following functions and activities: *List them.* You each expect to achieve the following results during the coming year: *List them.* You each expect the other to put forth at least a minimum level of effort on behalf of the business: *Specify hours, etc.* Assuming the business achieves what you expect it to achieve during the coming year, you will individually or jointly receive:

Specify compensation, etc. If you do *not* achieve the expected results, the following will occur: *List contingent plans for compensation, financing, additional effort, outside employment, etc.*

✓ **You agree that one of you will work for and assist the other in conducting his/her business.** The person who is assisting will be responsible for the following tasks: *List them.* The assistant will commit at least the following amount of time to the business: *Specify.* The boss will provide clear direction about how and when work is to be done, unless the assistant has the skill and experience required to be self-supervising. When the assistant does not satisfy the boss's expectations, this will be communicated promptly, clearly, and constructively, in a tone of mutual respect and appreciation for a good effort. The assistant will be compensated as follows: *Specify salary, bonus, time off, etc.* If this business arrangement does not prove mutually satisfactory, you will be honest enough to acknowledge this to each other, and you will make other arrangements. This will not be a rejection of your partner as a mate or as a living companion, only an accommodation to the needs of the business.

Structure of the Business

A closely held business can be in one of three forms: sole proprietorship, partnership, and corporation. The choice of form for the business can affect both of you, even if only one is the boss. Let's review them here.

Sole proprietorship. This is the simplest form of business. Only one person (the proprietor) is the owner. He or she does not receive a salary; instead, the owner is automatically the owner of anything that is left after the money has been collected and the bills have been paid. Debts of the business are automatically debts of the owner, and creditors have the right to demand payment out of the proprietor's non-business assets. The proprietor can have employees who *do* receive a salary, including the domestic partner; these salaries will be treated like other ordinary and necessary business expenses and can be deducted in computing taxable income.

Partnership. This form is an arrangement between two or more individuals (or, in some cases, corporations or other entities) to conduct business jointly. Good business practice requires that partnerships be conducted under a written agreement (the "partnership agreement") that spells out the rights and responsibilities of each partner. However, a written agreement is not required to form a legal partnership; merely holding yourself out to the public as partners is enough to have serious consequences. Partners are each *individually liable* for all the partnership's debts, so you can find yourself in deep financial trouble if the law regards you as a partner of an entity that owes money. In a *limited partnership,* one or more *general partners* will continue to have this unlimited liability, but *limited partners* are not at risk for any more than they have invested. A limited partnership must have a written agreement and meet other statutory requirements.

Corporation. This legal entity created under state law is distinct from its owners ("shareholders"). Shareholders are ordinarily not responsible for debts that are incurred by the corporation in the conduct of its business unless the shareholders separately assume the responsibility, such as guaranteeing the corporation's debts. Unlike the other forms of business, a corporation can survive beyond the death of its owners; the shares merely pass to the owners' heirs unless otherwise agreed. Corporate shares can be bought and sold, allowing ownership of the business to change while the underlying business continues undisturbed. (This is what the stock market is all about.) The price of all these benefits is strict compliance with state requirements, such as obtaining permits to do business; a separate level of income taxation (corporate earnings are taxed once when the corporation earns them and a second time when they are paid as *dividends* to shareholders); and the cost of maintaining corporate books and records, stock ownership records, minutes of board meetings, etc. *S Corporations* receive special income tax treatment from the federal government and some states: They are taxed like partnerships, without a separate corporate-level income tax. Instead, corporate earnings are treated as taxable income of the shareholders, regardless of whether the earnings have been paid to the shareholders or retained in the company. *Professional corporations* allow doctors, lawyers, accountants, and other professionals to obtain some of the benefits of corporate structure while practicing as regulated professionals. In these entities, only licensed members of the profession are usually allowed to be shareholders.

If you are going to work with your domestic partner it is very important that you understand the organization of the business. If the business is incorporated, there should be no problem; you have no ownership interest unless there are shares of stock registered in your name. If the business is a sole proprietorship, only the owner should be described as such, and nobody else's name should be displayed or advertised in connection with the ownership of the business. Unless you are the owner, your wages from a sole proprietorship should be reported to you on Form W-2 and then on your income tax return, while the net income of the business is reported on Schedule C or C-EZ of the *owner's* tax return. If you are a partner you should have a partnership agreement and should be given Schedule K-1 of the partnership's tax return telling you what income must be reported for your own taxes.

Under no circumstances should you allow yourself to be presented or described as owner of an unincorporated business except as a limited partner, unless you are willing to take personal responsibility for debts of that business. If you have any doubts, don't fool around. Either get a lawyer or get out.

An Outside Point of View

Nobody can think of everything, least so the time-pressed entrepreneur who is occupied with the day-to-day running of a business. No matter how talented a manager or producer he or she is, the successful business owner will seek the advice of other knowledgeable outsiders.

A business can draw on this outside expertise in one of two ways. First, it can establish a board of directors who have substantial relevant business experience, but who are not beholden to the business owner for their own livelihoods. These people can serve many roles, including a sounding board for the owner's ideas and a source of suggestions based on things they have seen work for other organizations.

The other source of outside information is the squad of professionals that serve the business. The business's lawyer, accountant, banker, insurance agent, and other professionals also have exposure to many organizations and can be a source of fresh ideas.

It is very important to get these advisors in place well before any ownership transition takes place. This way the outside directors and advisors will have a chance to get to know the business and learn how the current owner handles its problems. With the benefit of this knowledge, these people then can serve as advisors to the children or other new owners who later take over the business. In effect, the outside advisors can replace the owner's institutional memory and make the job of successor managers much easier.

Heir to the Throne

The family business is a unique enterprise. It almost always exhibits the character of its owner, and in many cases the owner *is* the business. The business becomes the owner's companion and child, and usually commands more of the owner's attention than the counterparts at home. Actually, some people probably join their mates in the family business because that is the only place to see them awake. Successful family businesses often reward their owners with a comfortable or even plush living, high status in the community, and a legacy to pass on to their children.

I often run into this situation: I am introduced to the owner of a successful business, and we begin to talk about the future. He (or she) has made plans to leave the business to his mate upon his death. Is the mate currently involved in the business? No. Are any children involved in the business? Yes. So why are children who are experienced in the business someday going to find themselves working for the owner's mate because of the owner's estate planning? When I ask this question I usually get silence rather than an answer.

Actually, there is an understandable reason for this arrangement. It involves the estate tax laws which we will examine in Chapter Ten. A successful business will usually generate a large estate-tax liability for the owner's estate, but this can be deferred until the death of the surviving spouse if he or she becomes the owner of the business. Note that I say "spouse" because the estate-tax marital deduction, as it is known, is available only to married couples (and then only when the receiving spouse is a citizen of the United States).

Bequeathing control of a business to an uninvolved, uninformed mate is at best another example of muddy thinking, and at worst a recipe for disaster and intra-family bitterness. What the business owner usually wants to accomplish when deciding who will run the business is the following:

✓ to provide sufficient income and capital to meet the lifetime needs of his or her surviving mate

✓ to provide control and, usually, ownership in the business to the child(ren) who are involved in it

✓ to be "fair" to children who are not involved in the business by giving them something equal in value to what their involved siblings receive.

A surviving mate can be provided for through the purchase of outside investments, life insurance, trusts, property that is leased to the business (giving the survivor a steady stream of income), or through limited partnership interests or non-voting stock that can generate cash payments without giving a voice in management of the enterprise.

An uninvolved child can be provided for with insurance, non-voting stock, a buy-sell agreement that allows the company to reacquire the child's stock at a fair price, or a "family partnership" that may hold interests in the family business or other assets, from which the child can draw financial benefits without exercising control.

Finally, the children who work in the business ought to get what they deserve: the financial rewards for their efforts through ownership and control of a business that, with time and success, will become increasingly valuable. The wise parent will also provide these children with what they need most in order to succeed: intangibles such as education, experience, appropriate responsibility, and mentoring.

Someone Else's Kids

What happens to the closely held business when your mate has children from another relationship? A lot of possibilities come to mind, and not all of them are very appealing. Consider the following case:

♠ CASE 1: Time for Some Changes

Kim had a young son from a brief earlier marriage when she met and moved in with Ann. They soon opened an art gallery together and spent the next twenty-five years making it a success. Kim's property settlement had provided the funds for starting the business, so she held a 51% interest and the title of president.

Kim's son Tim had a checkered academic career, flunking out of two colleges before graduating from a third-rate school with a bachelor's degree in art history. Six months after Tim's graduation Kim died in an auto accident. She left no will, so her 51% share of Reprise Gallery went to Tim, her sole legal heir. Tim lost no time in telling Ann that he wanted to increase commissions on art sales, double the cash allowance the owners received from the business, and close the gallery on Saturdays (its busiest day) so he could engage in sailboat racing, his hobby. Ann found herself arguing with him constantly.

After four months Tim informed Ann that she would not be welcome at the gallery any longer. She would continue to get distributions (49% of everything taken out of the business) but would effectively have no say in managing it. Ann tried to per-suade Tim that even though he did not like her, he needed her experience to balance his own youth. Tim would not hear of it. Ann left, and nine months later the company went bankrupt.

There were several problems in this case. Kim's failure to leave a will disinherited Ann, her domestic partner and the rightful heir to the business, in favor of Tim. The corporate bylaws did not guarantee Ann an active role in the business. And there was no buy-sell agreement between the shareholders, which could have forced Tim to sell to Ann or to buy her stock at a fair price if she was no longer to be allowed to work in the business.

A buy-sell agreement can avoid much litigation and grief. It spells out the terms under which an interest in the business (either a partnership or a corporation) can be transferred. Often it requires that departing owners sell their interest back to the business, or to other existing owners, rather than to an outsider who might disrupt the workings of the organization.

Keeping What You Make: Income Tax

In a legal system that is built around the traditional structure of marriage and family, it comes as no surprise that unmarried couples are taxed differently than their married counterparts. What *is* a bit surprising is the lack of consistency: In some cases unmarried couples are clearly the losers; in other cases, not.

In this chapter we take a look at the income tax system to find the opportunities and traps that await unmarried couples.

The Money Machine

In the eyes of the Internal Revenue Service you are a money-making machine. The Service, as tax professionals call it, does not much care whether you work for yourself or someone else, or whether your income comes from wages, pensions, or interest on the Swiss bank account your Uncle Elmo left you. It doesn't even care whether your income is legal or not. Many a gangster and drug dealer has gone to jail not for specific crimes against society, but for failing to report and pay tax on their ill-gotten profits. In fact, the Internal Revenue Code requires us to declare "all income from whatever source derived,"* subject only to specific exceptions that are written into the law.

Even machines need some tender loving care once in a while. The Service is willing to make allowances for those little things many of us insist on having while we go forth and profit: things like a child, an elderly parent—generally, our families. When we need to retain extra cash to support these *dependents,* the tax law obliges. And of course there is special treatment for our mates, at least if we are married to them. Married couples are viewed as a single economic unit (a valuable one, since one part can be earning cash while the other part gives the kids their baths) and are permitted to file a joint tax return. The only other taxpayers permitted to file jointly are, likewise, an economic unit: parent corporations and their subsidiaries.

Filing Status

The first question on the standard income tax return, once you have identified yourself, is your filing status: single; married, filing separately or jointly, or as an unmarried "head of household" if you meet certain qualifying tests. The tax code is rife with distinctions based on filing status.

One example is the standard deduction. Unless you itemize deductions, your standard deduction is subtracted from *adjusted gross income* (your gross income less certain items such as alimony contributions, retirement plan and Individual Retirement Account contributions, and portions of the health insurance and self-employment taxes paid by self-employed people) to compute *taxable income,* on which your tax is based. In 1994, the standard deduction for a single taxpayer is $3,800, while for a married couple it is $6,350. Since two unmarried adults would be entitled to a combined

* I.R.C. Sec. 61(a).

$7,600 standard deduction, this is one instance in which being un-married could be an advantage.

Filing status also determines what tax rates will be applied to your taxable income. Here are the official tax brackets for singles and married/joint filers in 1994:

SINGLE		MARRIED FILING JOINTLY	
Taxable Income	Tax Bracket	Taxable Income	Tax Bracket
0–$22,750	15%	0–$38,000	15%
$22,751–$55,100	28%	$38,001–$91,850	28%
$55,101–$115,000	31%	$98,851–$140,000	31%
$115,001–$250,000	36%	$140,001–$250,000	36%
$250,001–over	39.6%	$250,001–over	39.6%

These are called *marginal tax rates,* which means that the rate for your tax bracket only applies to income you earn that exceeds the limits for lower brackets. For example, if a single individual had taxable income of $23,500 in 1994, the first $22,750 would be taxed at 15%, and the remaining $750 would be taxed at 28%.

Here, again, the scales favor single people. Two individuals with equal incomes could earn up to $45,500 in 1994 without ever leav-ing the 15% tax bracket. If those same individuals were married, they would have paid a 28% tax on $7,500 of their combined in-come, because the 28% bracket begins for married couples at $38,001 instead of $45,501. However, each taxpayer is allowed a "personal exemption" which is $2,450 in 1994; the extra exemption in a married couple's calculation helps to reduce the marriage penalty.

We can see the overall effect in the following case:

▪ CASE 1: Starting Out

Jim and Joan graduated business school together and began identical jobs at the same company starting on July 1, 1994. They were also in love. Just after they began working they told Jim's ex-roommate, Artie, that they planned to get married sometime during the winter. Artie, who was just starting his own job with an accounting firm, offered to run some numbers for them to see if they should be married before or after the end of the year.

Here is what he came up with:

	SINGLE	MARRIED/ JOINT
Gross Income	$25,000	$50,000
Personal Exemptions	(2,450)	(4,900)
Standard Ded.	(3,800)	(6,350)
Taxable Income	$18,750	$39,100
Tax	$ 2,812.50	$ 5,910
Adjust for 2	×2	
Total Tax	$ 5,625	$ 5,910
"Marriage Penalty"		$285

Jim and Joan were very grateful to Artie for alerting them to the cost of getting married. As they were just starting out, they saw no reason to pay nearly $300 in unnecessary taxes when they could easily defer their wedding until 1995.

The "marriage penalty" has been a fixture in American tax law for many years. At one time a few couples made it a practice to obtain a foreign "divorce" every autumn so that at year end, when filing status is determined, they could pay a lower tax; they would "remarry" every spring. The Service cracked down on such shams and for a time in the 1980s Congress gave some married couples a special deduction to mitigate the marriage penalty. More recently, the tax legislation passed in 1993 effectively raised the marriage penalty for two-earner couples who are in the higher tax brackets.

The marriage penalty only tells part of the story about joint filing. Many unmarried couples would leap at the chance to file joint returns if they could legally do so. Joint filers enjoy many benefits, such as the ability to deduct one partner's business or investment losses against the other partner's income; the ability to combine and claim each other's itemized deductions such as qualified interest payments and taxes; and the ability to claim one another's *dependents.* (Dependents are discussed later in this chapter.)

While the tax system penalizes two-earner married couples with similar incomes, it rewards the traditional family structure that includes a married couple in which one person is the principal earner. Another case illustrates this marriage bonus:

↑ CASE 2: Wedding Bells and Elvis Flicks

Len was thirty-one, a successful insurance salesman earning $130,000 a year, and Liz was twenty, just completing her bachelor degree in premedical studies. Liz figured it would be at least six years before she earned a significant income. She and Len were confident that their relationship would hold up well under the strains of medical school, internship, and residency.

One day Artie, a classmate of Liz who was just completing his accounting degree, remarked to her that he thought it would be cheaper for Liz and Len to be married than to live together while she was in medical school. On the assumption that Liz would have no current income, Artie prepared the following estimate of Len's taxes if he remained single or if he got married:

	SINGLE	MARRIED/ JOINT
Gross Income	$130,000	$130,000
Personal Exemptions	(2,058)	(4,900)
Standard Ded.	(3,800)	(6,350)
Taxable Income	$124,142	$118,750
Tax	$ 34,331	$ 29,117
"Marriage Bonus"		$ 5,214

Upon seeing Artie's figures, Len booked two seats to Las Vegas, where he and Liz were married between sessions of the first annual Flying Elvis Film Festival.

In Case 2 you might notice that, as a single filer, Len's personal exemption was reduced from $2,450, as in Case 1, to $2,058. This is the result of a disguised tax increase that took effect in 1991. While the top tax bracket officially is 31%, taxpayers with incomes above certain levels lose some of the benefit of certain items including itemized deductions and personal exemptions. For single filers, personal exemptions begin to be reduced (for 1994 taxes) at an income of $111,800, while for married joint filers the exemption cutback does not begin until income reaches $167,700. For the traditional one-earner, married couple, the tax system makes certain that marriage pays!

Dependents

Homosexual couples cannot partake of the tax treatment available to married couples, since no state recognizes same-sex marriages. But can a gay couple at least have one partner claim the other as a dependent? Only in some circumstances. A taxpayer's claimed dependent must meet five separate tests described below.

Relationship test. The law requires that a dependent either be a relative of the taxpayer (under a number of relationships that are spelled out, including child, grandchild, great-grandchild, etc.; foster child or other child placed with you by an authorized agency for adoption; son- or daughter-in-law; parent or parent-in-law; grandparent, great-grandparent, etc.; sibling, half-sibling, step-sibling, or sibling-in-law; and, if related by blood, your aunt, uncle, nephew, or niece) *or* must be a resident of the taxpayer's household for the entire year. Gay couples can meet the member-of-household test most of the time, but there is a catch: This exception is not available if the relationship is in violation of local law. If you are a homosexual couple residing in a jurisdiction that outlaws homosexual relationships, you may not qualify under this test. (There may be a distinction between a local law prohibiting homosexual *acts* and one prohibiting homosexual relationships. As the courts have not ruled on this, we can only guess at the outcome.)

Can you do anything if you live in a jurisdiction where the laws are a problem? I can think of only three possibilities: 1) Move; 2) Try to legally adopt your partner (but get an attorney's advice on the potential legal consequences of having a sexual relationship with an adopted child!); 3) Try to get your local laws changed.

Income test. Your dependent cannot have income exceeding the exemption amount ($2,450 in 1994), unless that person is the taxpayer's child and is either under age nineteen or is under age twenty-four and a full-time student.

Support test. The taxpayer must furnish at least half the dependent's support during the year. There are exceptions for situations involving children of divorced parents and in which several relatives support the dependent under a multiple-support agreement.

Filing status test. If married to someone other than the taxpayer, the dependent must not file a joint return with his or her spouse.

Citizenship test. The dependent must be a citizen, national, or resident of the United States; a resident of Canada or Mexico at some time during the tax year; or an alien child adopted by a U.S. citizen or national.

Unmarried couples in which both partners work will generally not meet the income test and may not meet the relationship test. Thus, perhaps more often than not, claiming your partner as a dependent may be impossible.

More is at stake than just the $2,450 dependency exemption. If you pay medical or other deductible expenses on behalf of a dependent, you can claim them as itemized deductions; if you pay them on behalf of another individual, you generally cannot take the deduction (and if the payments are big enough, you may have to report a taxable gift).

Until some state recognizes same-sex marriages, homosexual couples and others who remain unmarried for personal reasons will have to do some careful planning to minimize the disadvantages they face under the tax law.

Capital Gains and Losses

Investments offer one area where a couple can benefit greatly at tax time from planning ahead. When you sell an investment for more than it cost you, you report a *capital gain.* An investment that sells for less than it cost you generates a *capital loss.* Capital gains from assets that have been held at least a year are presently taxed at a maximum rate of 28%, which under the tax law passed in 1993 has become a significant benefit for higher-income taxpayers.

On the other hand, capital losses are deductible by individuals only to the extent of capital gains plus another $3,000. In other words, if you have a capital loss of $20,000, no capital gains, and a salary of $25,000, your gross income for the year will be $22,000 ($25,000 less $3,000), and $17,000 of the capital loss will be deductible in later years.

Suppose Mark and Mindy lived together in 1994 and had the following results:

	MARK	MINDY
Salary	$40,000	$15,000
Capital Gains	$15,000	None
Capital Losses	None	(10,000)

If they were married filing jointly, Mark and Mindy would report salary of $55,000 and capital gain of $5,000 (Mark's gain of $15,000 less Mindy's loss of $10,000), for total income of $60,000. But as single individuals Mark will pay tax on the $55,000 while Mindy will pay tax on $12,000, since only $3,000 of the capital loss will be allowed to offset her $15,000 salary. Being unmarried, their gross income is $7,000 higher.

Mark and Mindy could have done better. It so happens that

Mark's capital gain came from the sale of some Bone-Dry Dog Food Inc. shares he had bought several years earlier. What if, instead of selling the Bone-Dry stock, he had given it to Mindy and Mindy then sold them? Mindy's *cost basis* (the amount subtracted from the sale proceeds to determine gain or loss) would have been the same as Mark's, so she would have recognized the same $15,000 gain. But she would have been able to use her entire capital loss to offset it, so that the couple's tax situation would have looked like this:

	Mark	Mindy
Salary	$40,000	$15,000
Capital Gains	None	$15,000
Capital Losses	None	(10,000)

Now Mark would have paid tax on only $40,000 of salary, and Mindy would pay tax on $15,000 of salary and $5,000 of capital gain. The couple's combined gross income would be $60,000, exactly the same as a married couple's. (The tax might still be slightly different because of different standard deductions and other variations, but the results would be close.)

Let's look at one more alternative. Mindy's capital loss came from the sale of some All-Wet Cat Chow Co. stock for which she paid $20,000 several years ago but which was worth only $10,000 when she sold it. Suppose, instead of Mark giving Mindy the Bone-Dry stock, Mindy had given Mark her All-Wet shares—would it make a difference?

Surprisingly, yes! Mindy's basis for computing gain or loss in the All-Wet shares was $20,000, because that is what she paid. But if she gave it to Mark at a time when the shares were worth $10,000 and Mark then sold them for that price, *Mark's* basis for computing the loss would have been only $10,000. There is a rule that says when property is received as a gift, basis for computing capital loss is the lower of whatever the giver's basis is, or the fair market value of the property at the time of the gift. If the couple had tried this strategy, here is what would have happened:

	Mark	Mindy
Salary	$40,000	$15,000
Capital Gains	$15,000	None
Capital Losses	None	None

This turns out to be the worst result of all. Because Mark's basis in the All-Wet shares is only $10,000, there is no gain or loss when he sells the shares at that price. Now Mark is paying tax on his combined $55,000 income, and Mindy pays tax on her $15,000 salary, for a total income of $70,000. Nobody ever receives tax benefit for the loss on the All-Wet stock.

Capital gains is one area where careful tax planning could save an unmarried couple a lot of money. When transferring assets between one another, you need to keep several things in mind. You are making a gift to the other partner, so these funds become his (or her) property; you need to be willing to accept that. And if you try to be too sly, by transferring property to a partner, having him sell it, and then having him give you back the proceeds, the chances are that the IRS would view the series of transfers as a sham and would tax you both based on the original ownership of the property.

Business Expenses

If you operate a business and your partner works there, you may have some real opportunities to reduce taxes. This is especially true if there is a large difference in your incomes, as shown in another case:

▪ CASE 3: The Employee

Barry owned a successful trucking company which was set up as an S corporation. The company earned $250,000 a year but paid no taxes of its own; Barry reported the income on his personal return.

Barry's domestic partner was Bobby, an aspiring actor and poet. Bobby worked at the trucking company during the day, contacting customers and coordinating drivers' schedules when he was not busy auditioning for plays and commercials.

Barry's accounting firm then assigned a new staff member, Artie, to do the trucking company's books and tax returns. After he got to know Barry and Bobby, Artie suggested that Barry put Bobby on the payroll as operations manager for $50,000 a year, plus a 15% profit-sharing contribution.

Barry took Artie's advice. As a result, Barry's tax bill dropped by $20,700 while Bobby's increased from zero to $9,293, for a net savings of $11,407.

Barry called the head of Artie's firm to compliment him on his fine tax advice, and Artie received an early promotion.

Interest and Dividends

If domestic partners have a large difference in income, it can be advantageous to put bank accounts, bonds, stocks, and other income-producing assets in the name of the person in the lower tax bracket. Under the *assignment of income doctrine,* you cannot simply designate another individual to receive income from an investment; you must give away the income-generating asset. This strategy, obviously, is suitable for the Committed Couple but never for, say, the Test Drivers.

Itemized Deductions

Although the majority of Americans claim the standard deduction, most individuals with incomes above $50,000 *itemize.* Itemized deductions are certain non-business expenses that you are allowed to subtract in computing your taxable income. The most important itemized deductions are state and local income and property taxes; certain types of interest; charitable contributions; medical expenses; casualty and theft losses; and certain miscellaneous deductions such as union dues, investment management fees, and some legal and accounting fees.

To claim an itemized deduction a taxpayer generally has to satisfy two basic tests: The expense in question must have been incurred by the taxpayer, and it must have been actually paid by that person. These requirements are not usually troublesome but they can be tricky for unmarried couples. The case below illustrates.

▪ CASE 4: The Homestead

Bert and Diane lived in a beautiful large home overlooking the Hudson River not far from New York City. The house was worth a lot of money and cost a fortune to maintain, not least because property taxes were $12,000 a year. But Bert was a successful author and was willing to pay the upkeep. The house actually belonged to Diane, who had inherited it from her grandmother's sister. Aside from Bert's agreement to pay the upkeep on the house, he and Diane kept their finances separate.

One year a routine IRS inquiry involving Bert's writing expenses led to a full-fledged audit. A young revenue agent, upon realizing that Bert did not own the house, disallowed the $12,000 property-tax expense as well as interest deductions for a home equity loan which Bert and Diane had used to finance a ski cabin. The agent also disallowed those expenses for the prior two tax years (which were the only ones still auditable under the statute of limitations), for a total of $66,000 in disallowed deductions. The tax bill totaled $30,000 when interest and penalties were included.

Bert's new accountant Artie glumly confirmed that the IRS agent was applying the law correctly. Next year, Artie suggested, Bert should give Diane the money and let her make the tax and interest payments on her own house, since they were legally her responsibility. Then she could take the deductions on her own tax return.

Let's take a look now at the major types of itemized deductions and at the special issues that affect unmarried couples.

Medical expenses. The high incidence of AIDS among male homosexuals has forced many unmarried couples to confront disastrous medical expenses. Legally, these expenses can often be confined to the AIDS patient and not his partner, but sometimes a partner may voluntarily spend large sums of money for medical care, drugs, private nurses, and other goods and services.

Unless the patient is a dependent of the partner (which is not likely, as we noted earlier in this chapter), these expenses are not treated as itemized deductions. In some cases, it may be advantageous to give the money to the patient and let him pay the expenses. This will not accomplish much tax saving, however, if the patient is so ill that he has little income on which to pay taxes in the first place. One bright spot is that if the healthy partner pays the doctors and hospitals directly, the payments are not treated as potentially taxable gifts. (We will discuss the gift-tax rules in Chapter Ten.)

In less extreme circumstances the deduction for medical expenses rarely matters anymore. Since 1987, these expenses have been deductible only to the extent they exceed 7.5% of the taxpayer's adjusted gross income. This level is usually reached only when a taxpayer is quite ill.

Interest. Once there was a simple rule: All interest expense was deductible. No more. Now interest is deductible only if it is incurred in connection with a business, certain investments, a mortgage of less than $1 million on the taxpayer's residence (the principal home plus one vacation home), or a home equity loan that does not exceed $100,000. Interest on *consumer debt,* such as credit cards and automobile loans, is not deductible.

One of the ironies of the 1986 tax reform which instituted these rules is that it classified education loans as consumer debt, making interest on them nondeductible, while allowing homeowners to borrow on home equity loans to fund college costs while deducting the interest. The idea, it seems, is that people who are fortunate enough to own their own homes deserve a tax subsidy for education costs, but other people don't.

As we saw in Case 4, it is important that the taxpayer who is deducting the interest be the one who is legally responsible for the debt and also, if the debt is deductible because it is secured by a home, the owner of the home. Joint ownership of the home is fine, since the loan will normally hold each homeowner fully liable for the debt.

State and local taxes. States use varying systems to raise money from their citizens. Not too many years ago federal law accommodated these differences by making most broad-based state taxes deductible, including income, sales, and property taxes. That changed in 1987 when the deduction for sales taxes was eliminated, leaving income and property taxes (on both real and personal property) as the major deductible state and local taxes. As is often the case, unmarried couples are at a disadvantage because an individual with a higher income cannot use deductions attributable to his or her partner.

Charitable contributions. Within certain rather broad limits, money and property (but not time or services) contributed to qualified charities can be deducted. Here, again, it is at least theoretically possible for an unmarried couple to run into problems if the individual making the donation is not the one who can best benefit from the deduction. In real life, however, I have seen few difficulties. There may be certain situations, though, when it will be better for one partner to give money or property to his partner, who can then retransfer it to a charity. If the retransfer is part of a prearranged scheme, however, the IRS would probably treat the contribution as coming from the first partner.

Casualty and theft losses. These deductions can be problematic for unmarried couples because of the inability to claim one person's loss against another person's income. The storms, floods, and earthquakes that have battered many parts of the nation in recent years are a good example. If one member of a couple owns a beach house and the other is the main income generator, very little tax benefit is available if the beach house is washed out to sea.

The basic rules to remember are: You can only deduct the amount that exceeds $100 plus 10% of the taxpayer's adjusted gross income; you can only deduct amounts that are not reimbursed from insurance or other sources; and you can only deduct an amount equal to the property's fair market value before the casualty or its tax basis, whichever is lower.

"Kiddie Tax"

After all this talk about how every taxpayer is responsible for himself, except for married couples who are treated as a unit, discussion of the "kiddie tax" rules may be understandably confusing. Back in 1987 Congress decided that the investment income of children under the age of fourteen should be taxed at their *parents'* tax rate if the kids have more than a minimal amount of income. Age fourteen was chosen, apparently, more for its revenue-raising potential than for any logic.

Basically, the rules work this way: The child is entitled to a standard deduction of $600 or, if greater, an amount equal to any *earned income* (wages, newspaper route earnings, etc.). Thus, if the child's income is $600 or less, the child owes no tax. Assuming the child has no earnings but has income from interest, dividends, and similar *unearned* sources, the next $600 is taxed at the child's normal rate, i.e., 15%. Kiddie tax kicks in once the child has more than $1,200 of unearned income. This income is taxed at the parents' marginal rate, not the child's.

If you are an unmarried couple living with a child under fourteen, the person who is the child's parent will be the one whose tax rate is used. If you are both parents of the child (either naturally or through adoption), and you are in different tax brackets, the higher tax bracket is used.

There are two ways to report and pay kiddie tax. The child can file his or her own tax return (Form 1040) and attach Form 8615; or, in certain circumstances, the parent (with the higher tax bracket, if there are two of you) can report the child's income on the parent's tax return (by attaching Form 8814 to the *parent's* return). Having the child file his or her own return will often produce a slightly lower tax liability, but this must be weighed against the trouble and expense of preparing a separate tax return for the child.

The kiddie tax rules do not seem to pose any particular hazards for unmarried couples. There are planning opportunities that apply to married and unmarried parents equally. Generally, these involve using investments that defer producing taxable income until the child reaches age fourteen and is taxed at his own rate. Some investments with tax-deferral potential are Series EE Savings Bonds, stocks with high growth potential but paying small current dividends, and cash-value life insurance contracts.

Planning Effectively for Income Taxes

One of the most frustrating (and common) experiences for a tax accountant is to have a client approach you a few weeks before April 15 and complain that his tax bill is too large. "Do something!" the client barks. The accountant usually shrugs, mutters something about the good old days when everyone could make a deductible IRA contribution, and tries to change the subject.

The time to do good tax planning is now—well, maybe even last week. The worksheet reproduced on the following page and in the Appendix will help you get a head start.

This chapter has illustrated some of the tax-planning issues unmarried couples face. There are many others; the tax law is too complex and personal situations too numerous to try to cover them all here. So, at the risk of sounding like an accountant who likes to drum up business (to which I plead guilty), I do urge you to get a competent professional to help you. Someone like Artie.

Income Tax Projections

NOTE: You can use this worksheet to compute your own tax liability (Column A), your domestic partner's liability (Column B), and, if you may be eligible to file jointly (i.e., legally married on the last day of the year), your joint liability. This worksheet provides only a rough estimate, especially at higher income levels; the tax laws are complex and subject to frequent change. Consult your own tax advisor for specific guidance.

Current values for tax rates, standard deductions, personal exemptions, and other amounts can be found in IRS Publication 17 or the instructions to Form 1040.

	Column A You	Column B Your Domestic Partner	Column C Filing Jointly
Gross Income			
Taxable Wages/Salaries			
Taxable Dividends and Interest			
Net Business Income (Loss)			
Net Capital Gain (Loss)			
Net Rent Income (Loss)			
Net Partnership Income (Loss)			
Other Income (Loss)			
Total Gross Income			
Adjustments to Gross Income			
Alimony Paid			
IRA Payments			
Keogh Plan Payments			
Other Adjustments			
Total Adjustments to Gross Income			
Adjusted Gross Income			
Itemized Deductions			
Medical			
Taxes			
Mortgage Interest Paid			
Other Interest Paid			
Charitable Contributions			
Casualty and Theft Losses			
Unreimbursed Moving Expenses			
Unreimbursed Employee Business Deductions			
Miscellaneous Deductions			
Reduction for Income Limitations	( )	( )	( )
Total Itemized Deductions			
Standard Deduction			
Greater of Itemized Deductions or Standard Deduction			
Allowable Exemptions (number)			
Allowable Exemptions ($ value)			
Total Deductions and Exemptions			
Taxable Income (AGI - Deductions & Exemptions)			
TAX (If you have capital gains, see instructions for Form 1040, Schedule D; otherwise use applicable tables or tax rate schedules.			

10

Keeping What You Have: Gift and Estate Tax

Our society seems to have a conflict about wealth. Judging from the number of lottery tickets we buy, most people would like to acquire large sums of money. We enjoy touring restored mansions, gawking at fancy neighborhoods, and generally seeing how the "other half" lives. But we are also a nation that shuns titles, cares little about social background, and prides itself on "equal opportunity." Many Americans just don't like the idea that one's station in life should be determined by whom one's parents happen to be.

Our estate- and gift-tax system grows out of this philosophy. The estate and gift tax has been carefully designed to apply only to a relatively small number of families, the ones with enough money to excite that American political instinct that loathes a family financial dynasty.

I have had the dubious honor of explaining the American gift- and estate-tax system to foreigners. The reaction usually ranges from incredulity to horror. While many other nations have estate or inheritance taxes, the American system is by many standards both broad-based and severe.

In this chapter we look at the gift- and estate-tax system and, particularly, at how it can work against unmarried couples. There is no doubt that being unmarried can be a great disadvantage in this area. Of course, most couples will avoid problems simply because their financial resources are modest. But if you are, or aspire to be, financially "comfortable" or "upper middle class," or better off than that, it is worth knowing how this tax works.

Taxing the Privilege of Giving

The United States has had gift and estate taxes for many decades, with numerous revisions. One of the most important changes came in 1976 when the two taxes were technically combined into a *unified transfer tax.* Since this change the two taxes have been, more clearly than ever before, a levy on the privilege of giving your property to someone else. At least theoretically, the two taxes are identical and operate in conjunction with each other. (We will see later that there are still some cracks that allow opportunities for tax savings.) And, usually, the tax is paid by the *giver,* not by the recipient. Money or property that you receive by gift or bequest is generally yours to keep without any income, gift-, or estate-tax payments on your part.

The unified transfer tax, like the income tax, is *progressive,* meaning rates go up as the amount being taxed increases. The system taxes only *taxable transfers,* which does not include everything you might think. Here are the rates that were in effect in 1994 for U.S. citizens and residents:

TAXABLE TRANSFERS	"TENTATIVE TAX"
Up to $10,000	18% of taxable transfers
$10,001–$20,000	$1,800 plus 20% of amount over $10,000
$20,001–$40,000	$3,800 plus 22% of amount over $20,000

$40,001–$60,000	$8,200 plus 24% of amount over $40,000
$60,001–$80,000	$13,000 plus 26% of amount over $60,000
$80,001–$100,000	$18,200 plus 28% of amount over $80,000
$100,001–$150,000	$23,800 plus 30% of amount over $100,000
$150,001–$250,000	$38,800 plus 32% of amount over $150,000
$250,001–$500,000	$70,800 plus 34% of amount over $250,000
$500,001–$750,000	$155,800 plus 37% of amount over $500,000
$750,001–$1,000,000	$248,300 plus 39% of amount over $750,000
$1,000,001–$1,250,000	$345,800 plus 41% of amount over $1,000,000
$1,250,001–$1,500,000	$448,300 plus 43% of amount over $1,250,000
$1,500,001–$2,000,000	$555,800 plus 45% of amount over $1,500,000
$2,000,001–$2,500,000	$780,800 plus 49% of amount over $2,000,000
$2,500,001–$3,000,000	$1,025,800 plus 53% of amount over $2,500,000
$3,000,001–over	$1,290,800 plus 55% of amount over $3,000,000

Based on this rate schedule you might expect most Americans to be very concerned about the unified transfer tax. This isn't the case, however, because of two critical freebies that are in the law: the *$10,000-per-recipient annual exclusion* and the *unified credit amount.*

The $10,000-Per-Recipient Annual Exclusion

The most generous break in the gift-tax law is a provision that allows each of us to give up to $10,000 per year, free of tax, to as many people as we want. An individual with ten children might (if she had enough money) decide to give them a total of $100,000 a year, every year until her death. Over a lifetime this procedure can transfer millions of dollars to heirs without generating a dime in tax.

This rule is even more generous when you consider that the recipients can invest the money they are given, and the growth of those investments will also escape transfer tax. Here is a typical case:

▪ CASE 1: Sharing the Wealth

Bernie was a successful businessman who enjoyed a close relationship with his three children, despite the fact that he was divorced from their mother and was living with another woman. When Bernie's children were still young (ages eight, five, and three) his business won a lucrative government contract and Bernie found himself with a large portfolio of investments.

Kathy, Bernie's investment counselor, suggested a balanced portfolio of 60% equities, 30% bonds, and 10% real estate. Bernie agreed, and he also liked Kathy's suggestion that he put as much of the equities and real estate into his children's name as possible. She established custodial accounts for them under the Uniform Transfers to Minors Act, with the children's mother as custodian.

Bernie placed $10,000 in each child's account on January 2 every year for the next twenty years. Kathy used those accounts to hold the most aggressively growth-oriented investments in Bernie's family's portfolio. The investments were quite successful, returning an average 18% annually during the twenty-year period.

At the end of twenty years each child's account contained $1,730,210. (Under the UTMA, the accounts had become the children's property outright when they reached age twenty-one.) Bernie had moved this entire amount to his children without paying any unified transfer tax.

A taxpayer in Bernie's position might have only one regret. Had he been married, Bernie could have made a "gift-splitting" election that would treat half of his gifts to his children as though they had been made by his spouse. That would have allowed Bernie to transfer *$20,000* annually to each child under the annual exemption, doubling the value of this technique. No gift-splitting election is available for non-spouse domestic partners.

The $10,000 annual exclusion is the biggest tax break available in the unified transfer system. It has come under some attack in Congress in recent years, as members have proposed limiting the total exclusions anyone could claim in a year to $30,000 or so. This restriction would not affect middle-class families (who obviously are unlikely to give away more than $30,000 very often) but would be a major setback to wealthy individuals who have numerous children, grandchildren, or other heirs.

For tax purposes, a gift that is excluded under the $10,000-per-year rule is treated as though it never happened. It never becomes part of the "taxable gifts" that are counted in the tax table set forth earlier in this chapter. It also does not reduce the amount of "unified credit" that the taxpayer can use to offset his first $600,000 of taxable gifts.

There are some limitations on the $10,000 annual exclusion. The most important is a requirement that the excluded gift be a *present interest* in something. In other words, if you put $10,000 in a

Swiss bank account for your child under an agreement that the money will go to the child on her thirtieth birthday, you have made a $10,000 gift but it is of a *future interest* rather than a present interest. The $10,000 will be counted as a taxable gift, although you may not have to pay tax due to the unified credit.

Hold it! What good is a $10,000 exclusion if it forces you to hand over the funds immediately to, say, your six-month-old daughter? Any sensible gift to a child will be of a future interest.

The law recognizes this problem. There are at least four reasonably good ways to make gifts to children, prevent them from gaining immediate control over the money or property, and still claim the exclusion. These techniques are: 1) gifts under the UGMA/UTMA; 2) gifts in a trust which requires that the children receive all the income from the property every year*; 3) gifts in a trust which *permits* but does not require the trustee to distribute income to the child, but which requires that the child at least have an opportunity to take control of the property upon reaching adulthood†; and 4) gifts to a trust which grants an opportunity to the child or his guardian to immediately withdraw the gift before it becomes subject to the trust's limitations on distributions.**

All of these devices allow you to make gifts to children in an appropriate manner and still claim the $10,000-per-recipient annual exclusion. Note that the exclusion is only available for gifts made during the giver's *lifetime;* it does not apply to bequests.

The Unified Credit

Although a $10,000-per-recipient tax-free allowance is fairly generous, an occasional bigger gift may arise in many families. It is not uncommon, for example, for middle-class parents to help children by providing the down payment for a home.

---

* These trusts are known as *Sec. 2503(b) trusts.*
† This type of trust is known as a *Sec. 2503(c) trust.*
** This withdrawal power is called a *Crummey power* and trusts that contain it are sometimes referred to as "Crummey trusts." Crummey powers are discussed in more detail in Chapter Twelve.

For purposes of these larger gifts, as well as for estate-tax situations in which no exclusion is available, another mechanism was needed if the unified transfer tax was to be targeted only at the truly affluent. This mechanism is the unified credit.

Technically, the unified credit is $192,800. This figure is the amount of gift or estate *tax* that is offset by the credit, so that no payment is actually required to be made. You can verify for yourself with the table above that a credit of $192,800 will exactly offset the tax on a total of $600,000 of taxable transfers. The case below illustrates how the credit operates.

⚑ CASE 2: Providing for a Partner

Betty and Veronica lived together for many years. Veronica, who came from a very wealthy family, wanted to provide for Betty's financial security. She gave Betty a Christmas gift of $10,000 every year they were together, and left $750,000 to her when she died.

In completing Veronica's estate tax return her executor made the following calculation:

Taxable Gifts During Lifetime	$ None
Taxable Bequests	$750,000
Total Taxable Transfers	$750,000
Tentative Tax (per rate schedule)	$248,300
Less Unified Credit	(192,800)
Estate Tax (payable by executor from estate's assets)	$55,500
Net Amount to Betty	$694,500

To verify his calculation, the executor observed that while the unified credit had avoided tax on the first $600,000 of Veronica's bequest to Betty, the remaining $150,000 was subject to a tax rate of 37%. The estate-tax payable of $55,500 is equal to 37% of $150,000.

Note that the unified credit allowed only once per *donor* (giver), rather than being available on a per-*donee* basis. The next case illustrates this, and points out one of the problems that may result.

▪ CASE 3: Who Pays?

Orville had two children by his brief marriage before he began a long-term relationship with Wilbur. Orville was quite close to his children Amelia and Lindy. Being financially successful, Orville gave each of the children $20,000 a year for the ten years before he died. At his death he left his entire $600,000 estate to Wilbur, feeling confident that no estate tax would be due because of the unified credit.

Orville's executor, Rudder, prepared the estate tax return and calculated the following:

Taxable Gifts During Lifetime:	
Amelia ($10,000 × 10 years)	$100,000
Lindy ($10,000 × 10 years)	$100,000
Taxable Bequests	$600,000
Total Taxable Transfers	$800,000
Tentative Tax (per rate schedule)	$267,800
Less Unified Credit	(192,800)
Estate-Tax Payable	$75,000

A quarter of Orville's taxable transfers went to his children because his annual gifts to them exceeded the annual exclusion limit. But although these children's gifts are what produced the eventual estate tax (by sending the taxable transfers above the $600,000 unified credit amount), the children did not bear any of the burden of this tax. Rudder had no way to assess a share of the estate tax against Amelia and Lindy, since they were not beneficiaries of the estate. Instead, Rudder reduced Wilbur's $600,000 bequest. Wilbur received $525,000, and the rest of the estate went to the government.

Had Wilbur and Orville been legally married the result would have been very different. Wilbur would have been able to use gift-splitting to exempt his entire $20,000 annual gift to each child from gift tax. Thus, his taxable estate would have included only the $600,000 bequest to Orville, and because of the unified credit, no estate-tax payment would have been due.

Many wills today do not use outright bequests to absorb the unified credit. Instead, these wills place an amount equal to the unified credit into a trust—(a *credit shelter trust* or CST)—for the benefit of children, domestic partners, or other desired recipients. This method allows the transferor to maintain some control over where assets ultimately go. For example, a $600,000 bequest to a domestic partner could be put in a trust that distributes income and principal to the partner during his or her life, but requires that any remaining balance at the partner's death go to the family of the original transferor rather than the surviving partner.

The $10,000 annual exclusion and the unified credit are the major tools for sheltering bequests to your non-spouse domestic partner. Unmarried couples are at a huge disadvantage, compared to married couples, because of the unavailability of the *marital deduction* discussed below.

The Marital Deduction

The American farm belt saw a tremendous boom in land values during the late 1970s. Even average farms were suddenly worth, on paper, several million dollars as the price of cropland soared to record heights.

For a time farmers found this boom helpful, as some sold and took the profits while others borrowed against the value of their land to acquire new equipment, or more land. But the skyrocketing farm values had devastating consequences when a farmer died and left the property to his spouse, who would then have to pay estate taxes. The law at that time contained a limited *marital deduction* which allowed only half the value of the spouse's estate to escape taxation, up to a maximum of $250,000. Farmers complained that to pay these taxes their surviving spouse would have to sell the family farm.

Congress responded in 1981 by enacting the *unlimited marital deduction*. Now, for the first time, the gift- and estate-tax law truly looked at married couples as an economic unit. The new law allowed the first spouse who died to transfer an unlimited amount of money and property to the surviving spouse without paying any tax. Of course, unless the surviving spouse spent or gave away all of this wealth, it would be taxed at his or her death, so the unlimited deduction served only to defer rather than avoid estate taxes. This deferred collection of tax was intentional.

The unlimited marital deduction immediately became the centerpiece of American estate planning. The following case shows why:

◢ CASE 4: All in the Family

Hal and Doris grew up on neighboring Minnesota farms, married and merged their parents' farms when they inherited them. They were diligent and fortunate and, over time, built their place into one of the most successful corn-and-hog operations in the state. They also raised two sons.

At Hal's death in 1982 the farm was worth $3 million, accounting for most of Hal's $3.5 million estate. There was no life insurance to pay the taxes. Fortunately, there *were* no taxes, because a month before Hal died his attorney Hubert had him change his will to take advantage of the new unlimited marital deduction. Hubert, who also served as Hal's executor, made this estate-tax calculation:

Taxable Gifts During Lifetime	$ None
Taxable Bequests:	
Investments (kids)	$500,000
Doris (farm)	$3,000,000
Gross Estate	$3,500,000
Less Marital Deduction	(3,000,000)
Total Taxable Transfers	$500,000
Tentative Tax (per rate schedule)	$155,800
Less Unified Credit	(192,800)
Estate-Tax Payable	$ None

Shortly after Hal's death the value of farmland in Minnesota and around the nation plunged. The farm, which had been worth

$3 million, was only worth $1 million when Doris died and left it to the children in 1989. Hubert made another calculation, this time for the estate of Doris:

Taxable Gifts During Lifetime	$ None
Taxable Bequests:	
Kids (farm)	$1,000,000
Gross Estate	$1,000,000
Less Marital Deduction	None
Total Taxable Transfers	$1,000,000
Tentative Tax (per rate schedule)	$345,800
Less Unified Credit	(192,800)
Estate-Tax Payable	$153,000

Hubert raised the money to pay the estate tax by selling some of the farm's assets to the children. They were in a position to purchase the assets from Doris's estate because they had cash left over from the $500,000 Hal had bequeathed to them years earlier.

Lacking a marital deduction or an effective substitute, unmarried couples are unable to defer estate taxes until the death of the second partner. We saw one example of the consequences back in Case 1 of Chapter One, in which the surviving member of a gay couple was forced to sell a cherished beach house in order to pay estate taxes.

Gay couples, in particular, probably will suffer for the lack of a marital deduction at least until some state decides to recognize same-sex marriages. The best anyone can do in the meantime is make good plans to cope with the tax burden.

What Is Included in the Taxable Estate?

We noted in Chapter Three that some assets (the "probate estate") are disposed of according to the deceased's will, while non-probate assets such as jointly owned property pass automatically by operation of law. To plan effectively for estate taxes one must first know the probable size of the *taxable estate,* which usually includes probate and non-probate assets.

The taxable estate includes:

All Property owned by the decedent at death. For a U.S. citizen or resident, this includes any type of property (including the value of intangibles such as copyrights and patents), situated anywhere in the world.

Property in which decedent had an interest. If the decedent was not the outright owner of property but had a legal claim on it, it is included in the taxable estate. For example, if the decedent owned 10,000 shares of Bone-Dry Dog Food Inc. at the date of death, and the company had (prior to death) declared a $1-per-share dividend payable three days after the date of death, the $10,000 dividend is included in the estate. This property is included because the decedent had a legal right to receive the dividend even though he (or she) had not collected it at the time he died.

Property over which decedent retained a life estate. This is an issue that can be important to unmarried couples. Suppose, for example, Rob wanted to ensure that his lover Les inherited Rob's house. Rob might change the deed to read that Rob is the owner as long as he is alive and Les is owner of the *remainder* after Rob dies. The retention of lifetime rights to use or enjoy property is called a *life estate.* Since Rob retained a life estate in the house, the entire value of the house is included in Rob's estate. (If this rule did not exist, the estate tax could be avoided simply by retaining only a life estate in all one's property, so that at the time of death there would be nothing left to tax.) Also included in this provision is property where the person making the transfer retained a power to designate who could enjoy the benefits of ownership. In our earlier example, this would apply if Rob gave Les the house outright, subject to a proviso that if Rob and Les broke up, Rob could designate a new owner.

Transfers taking effect at death. As in the rule cited above, this provision is designed to foreclose schemes by which property is automatically removed from the taxable estate because the owner made a gift of it, with the gift not effective until the owner's death. This rule also covers arrangements in which property is transferred to another person, when there is a significant possibility that the property could revert to the transferor. This situation might arise, for example, if you transfer property to your domestic partner under the condition that if your partner dies the property will automatically revert to you.

Revocable transfers. If you give an asset away but retain the right to revoke the transfer the asset is, logically enough, able to be included in your taxable estate.

Annuities. If the decedent bought an annuity that is payable to a surviving beneficiary, the value of that annuity is included in the decedent's estate. The next case provides an example.

♪ CASE 5: Retirement Benefit

Adele was a successful attorney in private practice. On her accountant's advice she created a retirement plan to which she could make tax-deductible contributions, knowing that she could benefit from tax-deferred growth and then take advantage of lower tax brackets when her working years were behind her.

Adele's domestic partner Barbara was financially naïve. Adele named her as beneficiary of the retirement plan, but she was still concerned that bad investments could leave Barbara in financial peril. So Adele invested $200,000 in an annuity that would begin paying benefits when she reached age sixty-five and would continue paying until she and Barbara were both dead.

Twenty years later Adele retired and began collecting the annuity. She was in poor health by that time, however, and died a year later. Thanks to twenty years of tax-deferred growth the value of the remaining annuity to Barbara, computed under IRS-specified methods, was $550,000. This entire amount was included in Adele's taxable estate.

Joint interests. This rule is of vital importance to unmarried couples. It states that when a decedent owns a joint interest in property (such as a joint tenancy), the *entire* value of the property is included in the decedent's taxable estate except to the extent that the remaining owners can prove they contributed to the original cost of the asset. The next case gives an example.

⚡ CASE 6: The Missing Records

Joel and Jeff became enamored of Central Florida during a visit to Walt Disney World in the early 1970s. Certain that the Orlando area would prosper, they bought a large parcel of raw land a short distance south of the city and held it as joint tenants.

Joel died twenty years later. At that time the land was the object of a furious bidding war by developers who wanted to erect a new resort outside the Universal Studios theme park. Officials at Universal also were interested in the property for future expansion. Joel and Jeff had paid $30,000 for the property in 1973; now it was appraised at $2.5 million.

The IRS insisted that the entire $2.5 million be included in Joel's taxable estate. Jeff, who was Joel's executor, argued furiously that he had paid half the original purchase price of the property, and so only $1.25 million was properly taxable to Joel. But the records of the property purchase had been misplaced and Jeff was unable to prove that he had contributed anything. The case went to Tax Court, and Jeff lost.

In this case the law again discriminates against unmarried couples. For a married couple, only one half the value of jointly owned property is included in the decedent's taxable estate, regardless of how much he or she contributed to the original purchase price. This treatment reflects the presumption that a married couple is a single economic unit regardless of whose efforts or checkbook is involved in a particular transaction.

For unmarried couples the response is clear: Keep scrupulous records of who paid for what, and keep those records in a secure place. If you cannot prove contribution, the result could be a *double* estate tax, since the same asset may be fully taxable in each domestic partner's estate.

Powers of appointment. People who use trusts for estate planning should be familiar with the way a *power of appointment* may result in an asset being included in an estate.

A power of appointment is a right to direct the payment of property by a trustee to someone else. If an individual holds a *general power of appointment*, that person is deemed to have an unrestricted right to use the property and must include all of the property in his or her own taxable estate. A *special* or *limited* power of appointment usually will not result in estate-tax inclusion. We will use another case as an example.

▲ CASE 7: A Matter of Control

Janie received a large property settlement and custody of her two small children, J.J. and Jill, when she was divorced from Pete. A few years later she met and moved in with Jesse. Jesse also had money, and Janie now felt that she was in a position to do something constructive for her children.

Janie asked an attorney to draw up a trust. Janie would contribute $1 million to the trust, which would require that the money be invested until both children had passed their twenty-sixth birthday; it would then be divided equally between them.

But Janie was worried that one of her children might have personal problems or special needs and so might not be a good candidate to receive a lot of money. She wrote into the trust that her trustee, Jesse, could change the beneficiary to a person of his choosing in his own sole discretion. Janie signed the trust, which was irrevocable, and paid gift tax because her $1 million contribution exceed the $600,000 unified credit amount.

Jesse died nine years later, just before the trust was to terminate. The fund had been well invested and by this time was nearly $4 million. The IRS demanded that Jesse's estate include and pay tax on the entire amount, even though Jesse was never a beneficiary of the trust. Why? Because although the trust did not make Jesse a beneficiary, the loosely written power of appointment gave him, at least technically, the ability to distribute trust assets to himself, his own estate, or his creditors. This language made it a general power of appointment and subject to taxation in Jesse's estate.

Janie, extremely upset, consulted a new lawyer. The lawyer told her that the trust language should have included a limitation to block Jesse from distributing the assets to himself or his own estate or creditors. For that matter, in Janie's situation, the power probably should have been limited so that Jesse could only reallocate funds between the two children rather than to another party.

Powers of appointment are a major issue in estate-tax planning and often are the focus of litigation between the IRS and taxpayers married or unmarried.

Life insurance. One of the most senseless, expensive, and common estate planning blunders I see is the mishandling of life insurance policies.

Life insurance death benefits, as we noted earlier in this book, are usually exempt from *income* tax. However, they will be subject to estate tax (as part of the insured person's estate) if the insured person had any *incidents of ownership* in the policy at the time of his or her death. Incidents of ownership include the power to designate the insurance beneficiary, the power to borrow against or collect policy cash values, and the power to surrender the policy or to exchange or convert the policy for another policy or contract.

More often than not, the person who is insured is the holder of some or all of the incidents of ownership. But this problem can be avoided by having another individual (for example, your domestic partner) be the owner of the insurance policy, or by having an irrevocable trust hold the policy. The trust can be written to pay benefits to your domestic partner only if, at the time of your death, you were still living together.

Existing policies can be removed from your taxable estate by transferring ownership to another person or trust, but this strategy works only if you survive at least three years after the transfer. There is no three-year tax exposure if a new policy is acquired directly by someone other than the person whose life is insured.

The three-year ''claw-back'' rule. We have now covered a number of methods by which previously transferred property can nonetheless be included in a taxable estate if the decedent retained certain control or *strings* over the property. The law seeks to shut down one further loophole. Suppose you placed all your assets into a revocable trust, for example, and left them there for five years. Then, while you were on your deathbed, you summoned your lawyer and had her amend the trust so that you no longer had the right to revoke it. Now it's not a revocable trust, so it is out of your estate, right? Wrong! The three-year "claw-back" rule brings the assets into your estate anyway.

The claw-back rule used to be very broad, declaring that any property transferred "in contemplation of death" was brought back into the decedent's estate. Today's rule is much narrower but somewhat complicated. It says that if property was subject to certain "strings" held by the decedent at *any time within three years prior to death,* the property is automatically included in the taxable estate.

The Gift-Tax Advantage

Based on our prior discussion of the unified tax system and the progressive nature of the tax, you might expect that taxable gifts and taxable bequests of equal amounts would bear the same tax. *It actually is much cheaper to pay gift tax while you are alive than to pay estate tax after your death.* The next example shows why.

♣ CASE 8: Better to Give Than to Keep

When Ellen's successful fashion company went public, she became rich. For the first time in her life she realized that there was no way she was ever going to spend the money she had made. Ellen had no children but she had a longtime lover, Connie, who was twenty years her junior. She decided to leave her entire $100 million estate to Connie and she hired a prominent estate planner to draw up the will.

Ellen's new lawyer told her that, from a tax standpoint, it would be better to give Connie a $50 million gift right now and pay some gift tax immediately. He drew up a simplified analysis, using a 50% tax rate and disregarding the unified credit and the $10,000 annual exclusion. Here it is:

	GIFT	BEQUEST
Initial Estate	$100 MM	$100 MM
Less: Gift to Connie	(50 MM)	None
Less: Gift Tax (50%)	(25 MM)	None
Remaining Estate	$25 MM	$100 MM
Less: Estate Tax (50%)	(12.5 MM)	(50 MM)
Bequest to Connie	$12.5 MM	$50 MM
Total to Connie:		
Gift	$50 MM	None
Bequest	$12.5 MM	$50 MM
	$62.5 MM	$50 MM

Ellen was confused until her lawyer pointed out that the gift tax is *exclusive* (the amount subject to tax does not include the tax itself) while the estate tax is *inclusive* (the amount subject to tax includes the money that will be used to pay the tax). The effective tax rate for gifts is therefore significantly lower than for estates.

Of course, Ellen had to consider some other factors. What if she gave Connie $50 million and they broke up? What if Connie died first without a valid will, or wrote a will but did not leave the money to Ellen? After much soul-searching, Ellen decided that the multi-million-dollar savings were worth these risks, and she made the gift.

The potential savings for paying gift tax rather than estate tax opens up another opportunity for abuse: People on their deathbed would make large taxable gifts to reduce the tax-inclusive amount that would otherwise go to their estate. The law prevents this last-minute gift-giving by adding another claw-back: Any gift taxes paid within three years of death are automatically added back to the decedent's estate.

Valuation Issues

When a gift or bequest is made in money or similar easy-to-value commodities, the computation of tax liability is fairly straightforward. But what about a bequest of shares in a family business? A copyright in a yet-unpublished novel? Undeveloped land?

All of these items (and all other property that is subject to transfer tax) are supposed to be measured at their *fair market value* —the theoretical price at which a willing buyer and willing seller would make an exchange, assuming each had available all the facts and neither was compelled to buy or sell.

So much for theory. In practice, if these hard-to-value items are worth anything more than a trivial amount, you will likely need to hire an appraiser. Getting a good, professional appraisal is one of the smartest things you can do when making a substantial lifetime gift, because in the event of a later dispute with the IRS about the value of a gift, your study (done at the time of the transaction) is going to carry more weight than an after-the-fact analysis performed by the IRS's valuation staff.

Sometimes, for transfer-tax purposes, things can be worth much less than they appear to be. One example expressly authorized by law is the *special valuation* that is available for certain farm or other real estate used in a closely held business. It is not uncommon for farmland to be worth much more as, say, a site for a shopping center than it could ever be worth for its crop-raising capacity. While normal valuation rules would require the highest value to apply, the special provisions allow the land to be valued at its farm or other current use assuming numerous technical requirements are met. Valuation is a very touchy and frequently litigated area of the law, so if it could apply to you, get expert help.

Another opportunity in valuations is the identification of various *discounts* that reduce value for transfer-tax purpose. Consider a 10% share of a business that is worth, all told, $10 million. Is the 10% share automatically worth $1 million? Probably not. First, a minority shareholder cannot unilaterally take money out of the business, fire the company president, or otherwise exercise control. Second, unless the stock is traded on a public market, it probably is not very liquid; you would have to incur significant costs in order to sell it. Buyers recognize these limitations and demand a discount to compensate. These *marketability and minority discounts* can be very significant, sometimes equaling 35% or more of the initial fair market value. But there is no set formula, only the weight of expert opinion (your expert's against the IRS expert's, that is).

Sometimes the value of an estate's assets will tumble shortly after the individual's death. This decrease could have severe consequences if the estate tax were fixed according to date-of-death values; the tax could end up gobbling the entire estate! To prevent this, Congress allows executors to use an optional *alternate valuation date* which is exactly six months following the date of death. If the assets have declined precipitously in that six-month period, the alternate valuation date can provide major tax-saving opportunities.

Income in Respect of a Decedent

Suppose that Irving, a salesman, closed a $10 million deal on Wednesday that earned him a $200,000 commission. On Thursday Irving suffered a fatal heart attack. On Friday Irving's executor wrapped up the estate, awarding Irving's domestic partner Pamela the right to collect Irving's $200,000 commission. On Monday Irving's employer gave Pamela the $200,000 check.

The general rule, mentioned earlier, is that property received by bequest or gift is not subject to income tax. There is an exception, however, for *income in respect of a decedent,* or IRD. IRD represents money that has been earned by an individual but was not collected until after the individual died. It is subject to income tax. The tax is paid by the executor or the beneficiary, depending upon who collects the IRD. Items of IRD are therefore subject to *both* the income and estate tax, although to mitigate this double taxation somewhat, an income tax deduction is allowed for any estate tax attributable to the IRD.

Typical large IRD items are balances in pensions and IRAs; other deferred compensation; commissions and similar payments; accrued income on savings bonds; and proceeds from sales of farm products, inventory, etc. Both the accounting and the tax-planning issues for IRD are very complex and, if the balances are significant, usually mandate professional guidance.

Non-Resident Aliens

We noted earlier that U.S. citizens and residents are subject to U.S. estate tax on all their property, wherever and whatever it is. The rules are different for nonresidents who are not U.S. citizens.

Obviously, our government cannot tax a citizen and resident of Switzerland on his Geneva villa just because Washington would like to raise some money. U.S. transfer taxes generally are imposed on non-resident foreigners only for property that is deemed to be situated in the United States.

Sometimes the definition is easy. Real estate is subject to U.S. transfer tax if the property is in the United States. (The gift or estate tax would apply regardless of whether the recipient is a U.S. resident.) Gifts of *intangible property,* such as corporate stock, are not subject to U.S. gift tax when made by a non-resident alien (unless that person had been a U.S. citizen within ten years prior to the gift), but stock in a U.S. corporation is subject to estate tax when owned by a non-resident alien decedent. However, in a departure from most economic wisdom, in this context currency is viewed as *tangible* property, making it subject to tax if the transfer takes place in this country (including at a U.S. bank).

Just who is a resident and who is a non-resident alien? This also is a gray area; the rules are much less cut-and-dried than in the income tax arena. The issue is essentially one of *domicile,* which is where a person's major personal and business connections are situated.

Non-resident aliens do not benefit from a $600,000 unified credit amount; they receive only a $60,000 allowance.

Other Provisions

Transfer-tax law is an extremely complex specialty. Congress has changed the law many times in the past two decades, often to promote "fairness" or curb some perceived abuse. For the present, the best advice is to review your overall situation and objectives in light of what we discussed in this chapter; the Estate Tax Projection worksheet reproduced here and in the Appendix will help you. If you have questions or concerns, and an estate big enough potentially to attract estate or gift tax, you ought to be talking to an expert. If you are like most people, you can look over the rules, add up your own balance sheet, and conclude that the gift- and estate-tax system is not an issue for you.

Estate-Tax Projection

Part 1: Compute Your Gross Estate

In this section you will compute the *gross estate*, which is the amount of property potentially subject to federal estate tax upon your death. Include all property owned by you and, if you are not married, all jointly owned property, unless your survivors can show you contributed only a certain percentage of the original cost. For example, assume you are joint owner of a piece of land worth $100,000 and the other owner is your domestic partner. If you cannot prove how much you contributed to the cost, include the entire $100,000 in your gross estate (even if you contributed nothing). However, if you can prove that you contributed only part of the cost, include only the portion of the value that reflects the percentage you contributed.

Gross Estate	Current Value
Liquid Assets	
Less: Life Insurance Cash Value	( )
Investment Assets	
Personal Assets	
Total Assets	
Short-Term Debt	
Long-Term Debt	
Total Debt	
Net Worth (Total Assets - Total Debt)	
Net Worth (computed above)	
Insurance on Your Life Owned by You	
Gift Taxes Paid in Last 3 Years	
Property Subject to "Claw-Back" Rules Within Past 3 Years	
Gross Estate	

Part 2: Compute Your Estate Tax

Gross Estate	
Less: Estimated Funeral Expenses	( )
Estate Administration	( )
Adjusted Gross Estate	
Less: Marital Deduction	( )
Charitable Deduction	( )
Taxable Estate	
Add: Adjusted Taxable Gifts	
Tentative Tax Base	
Tentative Estate Tax (from table on pages 152–53)	
Less: Unified Credit	($192,800)
Gift Taxes Paid on Lifetime Gifts	( )
State Death Tax Credit	( )
Other Credits	( )
Net Estate Tax	

The Price of Protection

We all face risk. Risk of losing a job; becoming ill, disabled, or dying prematurely; of being sued; of having our property damaged or stolen.

We manage these risks in different ways. Often, and sometimes quite foolishly, we ignore them. Sometimes we do what we can to minimize them (such as driving defensively), and sometimes we defy them (by racing cars, or drinking before driving). And other times we pay somebody else to take a risk off our shoulders—we buy insurance.

As a financial planner I view insurance as probably the most important money-management product around. It is also, unfortunately, perhaps the most misused, the most abused, and the least understood by the consumer. In this chapter we will take a look at key types and uses of insurance, and how to spend your premium dollars wisely.

Managing Your Risk

Why is an insurance company willing to accept your modest premium and shoulder the burden of a large loss? Because the insurance company lives by the *law of large numbers,* which essentially states that a certain random event will happen only a limited and predictable number of times in a given *population.* An insurance company has thousands of customers, so it has a large population over which to spread relatively infrequent risks.

For the law of large numbers to work, it is very important that insurance companies avoid *adverse selection.* Adverse selection is what happens when you allow people who already have suffered a loss (or who can clearly see one coming) to buy insurance to cover it. A life insurance agent could sell a lot of policies at a cancer institute or AIDS clinic, but no company would want to write the coverage. This risk is why life and disability insurers require physical examinations for individual applicants, and why auto insurers require photographs and inspection reports on newly insured vehicles. They need to avoid insuring losses that have either already occurred or become foreseeable. Physical examinations and other personal information is generally not required for policies covering large groups of people because, here, the law of large numbers provides protection.

A common insurance-buying mistake is for the consumer to believe that the law of large numbers applies to him (or her) *individually.* It doesn't. You are a population of one, so it is very little help, for example, to know that the life expectancy of a person your age is 83 years. *You* might just happen to live to be 102. As we will see later in this chapter, a lot of "permanent" life insurance that is sold will actually self-destruct if the individual lives beyond life expectancy. The financial consequences to that person's heirs will not be pretty.

Generally, insurance is most important and economical when it is purchased to cover a risk where the probability of occurrence is small but the magnitude of the potential loss is large. For a young person with large financial responsibilities, life insurance is the classic example.

Premature death and disability are examples of risks that have a low rate of occurrence (they seldom happen) and a large potential loss (when they do happen, they can be financially devastating). They are probably the two greatest individual insurance needs. (We covered disability insurance in Chapter Four).

Long-term care, such as nursing homes, is very expensive but many people need it, making suitable insurance quite pricey. An alternative is simply to build a good retirement financial cushion that can pay for nursing care if required, or to seek out less costly arrangements such as "life care" communities that provide certain assistance at a set price.

Life Insurance

Most of us think of life insurance as protection for survivors in case of premature death of a breadwinner. This is, in fact, the traditional and still the most important role of life insurance, but it is far from the only purpose. In fact, life insurance is used to accomplish all of the following:

✓ protect survivors from loss of financial support

✓ accumulate funds for retirement, college, and other long-term purposes

✓ provide ready cash to pay estate taxes

✓ produce a large estate with relatively low investment risk and a competitive aftertax return

✓ create a generous form of deferred compensation for business owners and key executives.

All this from insurance? Yes, thanks to some unique tax and investment characteristics of life insurance. But there is a catch.

The catch is that to get what you are paying for, you need to know much more about how life insurance works than most people ever actually learn. You should not rely on the insurance agent alone, though there are many well-trained and highly reputable insurance agents in the field today. Educate yourself or you could end up in an unhappy compromise: You pay less than you need to pay to get what you *think* you are buying, but much more than you should have paid to get what you are *actually* buying.

A case will help illustrate the problem:

▪ CASE 1: Here Today, Gone Tomorrow

Edith, sixty, was sole owner of a successful business worth $10 million. Her domestic partner, Sara, was not involved in the business and had no desire to take it over, but Edith felt sure that the value of the operation could continue to soar for many years with the management team she had installed.

Edith called Brooks, her insurance agent, and asked him for a policy that would pay a $5 million death benefit. This amount, she reasoned, would be sufficient to pay the estate taxes on the business, so that the stock could remain in Sara's hands if Edith died. Brooks asked a lot of good questions and realized that as the value of Edith's business increased, the policy death benefit would have to rise in future years to keep pace.

While Brooks went to work, Edith told her attorney, Douglas, to draft an irrevocable insurance trust that would actually own the policy (keeping the death benefit out of Edith's taxable estate). Everything seemed set.

Edith was shocked at Brooks's proposal: an annual premium of $125,000 a year for life! If Edith lived just twenty years, which was her life expectancy, she would pay total premiums equal to half of the $5 million death benefit. Brooks tried to point out that in twenty years the death benefit could double to $10 million if dividends were paid as projected. But Edith told him to keep the premium to $75,000, tops.

Three days later Brooks was back with a $5 million policy costing $75,000 a year. Edith did not notice the disclaimer buried on page five of the proposal which pointed out that under the proposed premium and projected interest rates, the policy would lapse in twenty years. Edith thanked Brooks and signed the papers to put the policy into the insurance trust.

Two years later Attorney Douglas attended a seminar in which the speaker said many policies designed the way Edith's was were underfunded and would not stay in force if the insured person lived beyond his or her statistical life expectancy. Douglas reviewed the papers on Edith's trust and, unhappily, called to tell her that they had made a very ill-advised purchase. If Edith happened to live beyond age eighty the policy would lapse and her premiums, which by then would have totaled $1.65 million, would go down the drain. On the other hand, canceling the policy now would be very expensive, since the insurance company was going to refund only $70,000 of the $150,000 in premiums that had been paid to date.

Edith told Brooks to update the original proposal; she would give the trust more money to buy that policy instead. At her suggestion the trustee (Douglas) exchanged the policy Edith's trust had first purchased, plus a new cash contribution from Edith, for the policy Brooks had recommended in the first place.

If you think this case is an extreme example of what can go wrong you are mistaken. These types of policy mistakes happen constantly. Perhaps the only unusual aspect of the case is that someone (other than the insurance agent) recognized the error after only two years had passed, and that the consumer belatedly realized that the smartest thing to do was admit a mistake and pay more.

To make an informed life insurance purchase you must understand the differences between the various types of life insurance products. The table below, and the discussion on the following pages, will give you an overview.

Product	Description	Best Uses	Benefits	Drawbacks
Term Life	Pure death protection	Protect family finances	Lowest premiums per dollar of insurance	Usually lapses without paying benefit
Whole Life	Usually level premium for life	Short-term death protection; long-term investment	Cheaper over long periods than term insurance	Substantially higher initial premium than term insurance
Universal Life	Hybrid; combines term insurance with a separate investment fund	Invest funds on tax-deferred basis	Flexible premiums	Not always designed to last for lifetime of insured
Variable Life	Whole life, but insured directs how premiums are invested	Invest funds on tax-deferred basis	Opportunity to share in superior investment returns	Often higher costs and less predictable insurance coverage than whole life
Variable Universal	Universal, but policy owner directs how separate fund is invested	Invest funds on tax-deferred basis	Essentially acts as a tax-deferred mutual fund	Higher costs than typical mutual funds; less predictable insurance coverage than whole life

Term life. This is "pure" death protection and is the cheapest form of life insurance. In a term plan, the insurance company collects a premium (usually annually) and promises that if the insured dies during the premium's effective period, the company will pay the stated death benefit to the policy beneficiary.

At the end of a year another premium is due. Since the insured will be one year older, the risk of death during the coming year is slightly higher than it was originally, so the premium for the second year may be slightly higher than for the first. Many term policies have arranged premiums in a "stair-step" or a "level" pattern, so that premiums do not rise for a certain number of years, or even for the life of the policy. These policies artificially inflate premiums in the early years in order to hold them down in subsequent years.

A term policy is usually *automatically renewable,* meaning the policy can be renewed regardless of deterioration of the insured's health, merely by continuing to pay premiums. However, there are liable to be two significant restrictions. First, automatic renewal stops at a certain age, often age seventy or seventy-five. If the insured dies after that age, he (or she) will not be covered. Second, many companies have recently added *reentry* provisions to their policies. After a certain number of years the insured is required to present new evidence of good health; otherwise the policy is either canceled or subjected to a massive increase in premiums. By imposing this requirement, the company subtly shifts some of the risk back onto the insured.

Term insurance plans often include a *conversion option* which allows the insured to exchange the policy within a certain period of time for a *permanent* whole or universal life policy. Exercising a conversion option usually requires a large onetime payment to make up for the difference between the lower term premiums that have been paid since the policy was established and the larger premiums that would have been collected had it been a permanent policy from the outset.

Term policies *do not accumulate any cash values.* The premiums that are discussed when the policy is sold (usually described as "current" premiums even though they show an increase during future years) are not guaranteed; if the insurance company's mortality or investment record is not as good as it expected when it sold the policy, it can raise the premiums later. Term policies do, however, show a maximum premium which is the highest amount the insurance company is allowed to charge under the contract. This "guaranteed" premium is often several times higher than the quoted "current" premium.

Term is usually the best type of insurance to get when the primary goal is to protect survivors' financial security in case a breadwinner dies prematurely. The low premiums make it easier to afford to buy adequate protection. But, of course, most breadwinners *don't* die prematurely, and most term policies never pay any death benefit. Because these policies have no cash value and only rarely are held long enough to pay a death benefit, they usually generate no financial return. Although premiums for other types of policies are much higher, those other policies have cash values that often make them cheaper to hold in the long run than term. Generally, if you anticipate keeping insurance in place for more than ten to fifteen years and can afford the higher premiums for other types of insurance, term is not the best choice.

Whole life. Whole life insurance is so traditional and so basic to the insurance industry that it is often called *ordinary life.* But there is nothing ordinary about the financial characteristics of this product.

When you buy a whole life policy, you are giving your premium dollars to the insurance company to invest on your behalf. The company will usually invest the funds in a diversified mix of fairly conscrvative investments (but not in low-yield instruments like tax-free bonds). You keep making premium payments every year, and the insurance company keeps making investments for you. Finally, when you die, the insurance company pays the investment proceeds to your family—*tax-free!*

By using the insurance company as an intermediary, the tax law allows us to escape taxes on what would otherwise be a fully taxable portfolio of investments. With properly designed whole life there is never any doubt about whether the death benefit will be paid; the policy is designed to last a lifetime.

Whole life can be a great deal, but there is a big *if:* You have to keep the policy in force for life in order to get the full tax benefit. If a whole life policy is cashed in while the insured is alive, the amount received by the policy owner is taxable to the extent it exceeds premiums paid.

What is *cash value* (sometimes called *surrender value*)? It is a return of the policyholder's own money. Cash value is created in an insurance policy in order to shift gradually the financial risk of death from the insurer to the policy owner. While this sounds a little sinister, it is in fact very natural and desirable, and it is the only thing that makes "permanent" insurance possible. The following case will show how whole life works when it is designed properly.

▪ CASE 2: A Lifetime Investment

Joe, age forty, had two young children and felt that they would need $1 million for their support and education if he were to die. Joe asked his insurance agent, Brooks, for some quotes, and Brooks told Joe that the Big Insurance Company would sell him a term policy for $1,000 a year, or whole life for $8,000 a year. Each policy would pay $1 million at his death.

Brooks showed Joe the following analysis to help him make his decision:

Year	TERM Premium	WHOLE LIFE Premium	WHOLE LIFE Cash Value
1	$1,000	$8,000	None
2	$1,050	$8,000	$6,300
3	$1,100	$8,000	$13,300
4	$1,150	$8,000	$21,000
5	$1,200	$8,000	$30,000
6	$1,250	$8,000	$40,000
7	$1,300	$8,000	$51,000
8	$1,350	$8,000	$63,000
9	$1,400	$8,000	$76,000
10	$1,450	$8,000	$90,000

Brooks pointed out that, if the policies performed as projected, after eight years Joe's net cost of owning the whole life policy would be only $1,000 (eight years of $8,000 premiums, or $64,000, less $63,000 surrender value), while by that time term premiums would have totaled $9,400. For the full ten years, term premiums would cost $12,250, while the whole life could generate a $10,000 *gain* ($90,000 surrender value less $80,000 total premiums).

Joe could afford to pay $8,000 annual premiums, but he was concerned that in later years the policy might become prohibitively expensive to maintain. Brooks then prepared a chart to illustrate the workings of the whole life policy:

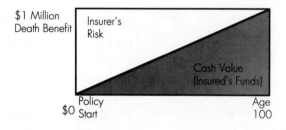

Over time, Brooks explained, the cash value of the whole life policy gradually provides an increasing part of the death benefit, reducing the insurer's risk. This allows the policy's premium to remain a steady $8,000 per year for life, for although the risk of death will increase as Joe ages, the amount of the *insurer's* money that must be paid upon his death will decrease. At age one hundred the cash value will equal the entire policy death benefit. The policy is said to *mature* or *endow* at this point, and the insurer no longer has any of its own money at risk; the insurance policy has become no more than a tax-favored savings account.

Joe now felt he understood how the whole life policy worked, and he bought it.

Note that in the case above the whole life policy gained no cash value in the first year, although the premium was obviously many times higher than the amount needed to provide the first year's death benefit. Where did the money go? Mainly, to Brooks—insurance agent commissions typically are 55% to 100% of the first year's premiums, with much smaller amounts in later years. With certain insurers, it is possible to use a sophisticated policy design to reduce this front-end cost and greatly increase the policy cash values, often by 50% of the first year's premium.

Universal life. In the late 1970s, insurers began promoting universal life, a product that basically married term life insurance to a short-term investment fund. Within broad limits, buyers of universal life can adjust coverage amounts and annual payments. Any payments in excess of the term insurance premiums are deposited into the investment "side fund." This side fund allows the policy-holder to accumulate earnings that are untaxed until they are withdrawn (if the insured is still alive) or completely tax-free (if the proceeds are paid at the insured's death). Universal life quickly gathered more than a one-third share of insurance sold, although this has dropped to a little over 20% in recent years as interest rates fell back.

Universal life is most valuable as a vehicle for accumulating funds over a period of ten years or more, since the tax-deferral feature allows the money to grow faster. But this must be balanced against the substantial costs of universal products, which can include sales charges at inception or when the policy is cashed in.

Universal life is considered "permanent" insurance because it can be renewed indefinitely. However, the minimum charge (the term insurance component) rises steadily with the advancing age of the insured. When the policy owner's premiums are no longer sufficient to pay these charges, the investment fund is invaded to make up the difference. Once the investment fund is exhausted, the policy will lapse or premiums must be increased dramatically. The chart below illustrates how this happens:

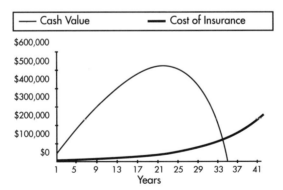

The cash value of the universal life policy increases for the first twenty-four years of the policy, at which time the annual cost of insurance begins to exceed the premiums that the policyholder is paying. The difference is taken from the investment fund, which begins to decline. In year 34 the investment fund has been depleted, the annual premiums have skyrocketed to the six-figure level, and the policy "self-destructs."

Variable life. Another modern product, variable life allows the policy owner to direct the types of investments in which the cash values are placed. If investment results are good, the policy's death benefit can be adjusted upward; death benefits may be reduced if investments fare poorly.

Variable universal life. This is a universal life policy in which the investment fund can be moved among various investments (often, a set of mutual funds run by the insurance company or another sponsor) ranging from very conservative to very aggressive.

Modified Endowment Contracts

In the late 1980s, insurance companies began touting their products' tax advantages very aggressively. Congress quickly stepped in with a new set of rules designed to make certain that life insurance products actually have a significant risk-transfer component rather than being a disguised investment vehicle.

Policies that fail one, relatively lenient, set of tests will not even be taxed as life insurance; death benefits will be fully taxable when paid, and "inside buildup" (the annual increase in policy cash values) will be taxable annually. It is very unusual for a policy offered by a major insurance company to fail to meet the definition of life insurance for tax purposes.

A stricter set of tests classifies certain policies as *modified endowment contracts* (MECs). A MEC is taxed as life insurance as long as cash remains in the policy. A death benefit paid under a MEC is generally tax-free to the recipient. However, certain transactions that have no tax consequence for conventional policies (such as borrowing against the policy's cash value) can create income tax liability from a MEC. Further, if these taxable distributions from a MEC are received by an individual under age $59\frac{1}{2}$, they can be subject to an additional 10% penalty tax.

The tests for determining whether a policy is a MEC are very complex and, as a practical matter, can only be performed by the insurer. MEC status is usually triggered when policy cash values are unusually high when compared to the policy death benefit, a computation that must take into account the insured's age and other actuarial factors. For some policies it may be necessary to perform calculations every year to ensure that such policies don't become MECs; corrective action, such as a reduced premium or increased death benefit, may be needed.

A term life policy cannot be a MEC because it does not have any cash values.

Insurable Interest

To receive the tax benefits of life insurance a policy must be treated as insurance under state law. State law will, in turn, require that the policy owner have an *insurable interest* in the life of the insured. Insurable interest is a very old requirement with a very practical basis: If people could buy insurance on the lives of strangers or casual acquaintances, bad things might tend to happen to those strangers. The law generally recognizes insurable interest on the part of oneself; one's spouse or other close relatives; partners, employers, and others in a close business or personal relationship.

Some unmarried couples may face a potential trouble spot, however. If a relationship is in violation of local law (such as a homosexual relationship in jurisdictions that prohibit such relationships), it is at least possible that a court would find the domestic partner has no insurable interest, because granting an insurable interest would be against public policy. It is even possible that the IRS would make this argument to deny a life insurance tax exclusion without a local court's having ruled on the question.

There are at least two possible ways to plan around this contingency if you are involved in a relationship that is arguably against local law. First, the insured can be the owner of the policy, since an insured always has insurable interest in himself. The domestic partner would be only the beneficiary, and this should pose no problem. This arrangement is simple and practical and should be used for insureds whose total estate, including the life insurance death benefits, is less than $600,000. It could be costly to use this method for larger estates, however, because by giving the insured ownership of the policy we bring the death benefit into the taxable estate. (This was discussed in Chapter Ten.)

An alternative is to place the insurance policy in a trust whose beneficiary is the domestic partner. If possible, I would have the trust enter into some sort of business arrangement with the insured, such as a partnership that owns a rental real estate property. As partner of the insured the trust would therefore have insurable interest without regard to the relationship between the insured and his domestic partner. I would favor this arrangement when the insured's estate (including the life insurance policy) would be more than $600,000.

Choosing an Insurance Company

In all this discussion of product design, legal and tax issues, we have not yet touched on the most important insurance purchase consideration of all: the choice of an insurance company.

When you buy insurance you are buying a promise. That's all you get, except perhaps for a golf outing with the agent and a simulated leather binder to hold your policy. You are going to hand over large amounts of money in return for the company's assurance that it will be ready, willing, and able to pay the promised benefits to your beneficiaries. How do you know with whom to do business?

Until recently few consumers gave much thought to this issue. In the early 1990s, however, we saw several large insurance company failures (Mutual Benefit and Executive Life being the most notorious) and many other companies report weakened financial condition, mainly due to bad real estate or junk bond investments. Fortunately, things have settled down a bit.

There are two key considerations in selecting an insurance company: *solvency* and *efficiency*. Solvency relates to the company's ability to pay benefits when due. Despite the highly publicized failures, insurance companies collectively have a very good long-term record of meeting their obligations. *Efficiency* measures how well a company can generate value for its policyholders, meaning paying the largest benefits for the smallest premiums.

Solvency is what is measured by the agencies that assign ratings to insurance companies. A top rating from these companies—A.M. Best, Moody's, Standard & Poor's, and Duff & Phelps are the major ones—means their analysts believe it is extremely unlikely that the insurer will default on its contractual obligations. These ratings say nothing, however, about a company's past or future efficiency. An insurer can be very inefficient and very solvent at the same time, such as by charging excessive premiums and keeping the cash in low-yielding Treasury obligations.

An annual study of major companies' ten- and twenty-year track record in delivering policy value is published in *Best's Review* magazine every summer. This ranking is the most accessible report that attempts to measure efficiency.

Policy Dividends

Closely related to the subject of efficiency, and the subject of much controversy, is the insurance industry's practice of projecting future policy *dividends.* When a whole life policy is issued, the insurer makes certain assumptions about its future investment results, mortality claims, and other expenses, and uses those assumptions to set the policy premiums. If, as has been the case most of the time, the actual experience is better than the assumptions, some of the "excess" premium that has been collected is returned to policyholders through policy dividends. These dividends can usually be taken in cash, held by the insurance company on the policyholder's behalf (the policyholder is paid interest on this money), used to reduce ongoing premium payments, or applied to buy additional insurance ("paid-up additions").

The insurance illustration is a multi-page spreadsheet brandished by the agent to demonstrate how a policy may perform. Illustrations usually bury, and sometimes ignore, the performance that the insurance company guarantees. Instead, it purports to be a more realistic estimate of likely performance. *Insurance illustrations are worthless for comparing one company's policy to another.* Often the illustrations are of little value even in comparing two contracts from the *same* company.

A few years ago some consumers and their advisors (myself included) began automatically asking agents to show alternative illustrations of what would happen if companies' investment earnings were several percentage points lower than the main illustration assumed. At first, these alternative illustrations showed significant drops in dividends. More recently the differences have been minimal.

What happened? In making assumptions about future dividends, some companies have apparently become less aggressive on investment returns because they know this is going to be scrutinized. It appears that at least some have compensated by becoming *more* optimistic about future mortality and other expenses.

Judging a company's future efficiency by its past track record (such as the *Best's Review* report) is a bit like driving by looking at the rear-view mirror. In many cases, however, it is the best we can do. Companies have historically been quite consistent; those that have long track records of doing well by their customers have tended to maintain their positions. We have to look at the record, make our best judgments, and remember that if something sounds too good to be true, it usually is.

Life Insurance Issues for Unmarried Couples

Members of unmarried couples have as much reason to buy life insurance as anybody else who is involved in an important financial or personal relationship. If the death of a partner would result in significant economic loss, then you should consider life insurance.

Life insurance also offers a way to mitigate the tax and legal disadvantages that an unmarried couple must face. A married couple, for example, can rely on intestacy law (though it should not) to make certain that the surviving partner receives at least a major share of the decedent's estate. The married couple also benefits from the unlimited estate-tax marital deduction, which for most couples ensures that no tax is payable at the death of the first partner.

Unmarried couples lack these advantages. What can they do instead? The next case provides an illustration.

▲ CASE 3: Planning Ahead

Sal and Craig expected to spend the rest of their lives together, had consolidated most of their finances, and were well accepted by each other's families. Both had good jobs, although Sal had started with considerable wealth from his family and earned much more than Craig. Sal would have no trouble handling the couple's financial obligations alone if anything were to happen to Craig, but Craig would need considerable help if he survived Sal.

Sal shared his concerns with Brooks, the insurance agent, and Brooks put Sal in touch with a prominent estate planner, Attorney Barney Douglas. Barney suggested the following plan:

✓ Sal would create an irrevocable trust with Craig and Sal's parents as beneficiaries. The trust would allow Sal to transfer as much as $30,000 annually to the trust under the $10,000-per-donee gift-tax exclusion.

✓ With Sal's first $30,000 gift, the trustee (Barney himself) would acquire a whole life insurance policy on Sal's life. At Sal's death the policy would be payable to the trust.

✓ The trust would stipulate that if Craig and Sal were still living together at Sal's death, Craig would receive the proceeds and the trust would terminate. If Craig and Sal were not living together at Sal's death, or if Craig died before Sal did, the death benefit would be paid to Sal's parents or, if they were no longer alive or the trustee believed it would be unwise to distribute the money to them, to Sal's siblings and their children.

Sal was delighted with the plan. It provided protection for Craig in the short-term, a large tax-free bequest to him in later years (because the insurance policy would be outside Sal's taxable estate), and benefited Sal's family in the event he and Craig were to separate or Craig did not survive Sal.

All that remained was for Brooks to present a whole life policy from a well-managed, top-rated insurance company with a good record of delivering value for policyholders. Brooks prepared proposals for four different companies, and after doing some research, Barney, as trustee of the insurance trust, made his selection.

Liability Insurance

We began this chapter by noting that risk is part of everyday life. That fact has not stopped or even seemed to slow down the explosive growth of litigation that seeks to hold various parties responsible for all sorts of happenings.

A hurricane blew the roof off your house? Sue the builder. A company whose stock you bought goes bankrupt? Sue the management, or the company's accountant, or your broker, or all three. A terrorist bomb destroys an aircraft that is carrying your relative? Sue the aircraft manufacturer for failing to build a bomb-resistant airliner!

Suits like these and many that are still more outlandish pile up in our courthouses like leaves on a forest floor. Regardless of their merit (and many indeed *have* merit), they are easy to file, expensive to defend, and often very costly for defendants who lose.

In this environment personal liability insurance is a necessity if:

✓ you have any significant assets (even a car, if it is reasonably valuable and not subject to a large outstanding loan)

✓ you have considerable potential future income, such as a medical or law degree

✓ you stand to acquire large sums of money, or the right to substantial income, at unpredictable times such as via bequests.

Personal liability coverage is a way of protecting what you have against claims arising out of injuries that you may inflict on someone else.

Most individuals acquire liability coverage through one or more of three sources: an *endorsement* (addition) to a homeowner's insurance policy; automobile insurance policies, and an additional *umbrella* liability policy.

The standard homeowner's (or renter's) policy endorsement creates the equivalent of a *comprehensive personal liability* (CPL) policy. Despite the name, this type of liability coverage is not truly comprehensive. The most important exclusions are liability arising from business and professional pursuits and from use of a car, plane, boat, or other vehicle.

Spouses are automatically covered by policies regardless of who owns what. But this is not true of unmarried couples. Check with your agent; it may be necessary either to put both partners' names on a single policy or to acquire two separate policies.

An umbrella policy is used in conjunction with some other type of liability insurance. Suppose you maintained $1 million in liability insurance on your homeowner's policy but, as partner in a big law firm, felt that your earning power and net worth required $5 million of coverage. You would seek a $5 million umbrella policy. This policy would pay only on claims that exceed $1 million; smaller claims would be handled entirely by the homeowner's policy. Depending upon how property ownership and underlying insurance is arranged, unmarried couples may have to take extra steps to procure adequate umbrella coverage.

Property Protection

Fires, thefts, natural disasters—all sorts of threats imperil our property. The homeowner's insurance policy is the basic form of financial protection for these assets, even for people who do not own a home.

The most popular form of homeowner's insurance today is the *all-risk* form of coverage (HO-3, in insurance company language). Despite the name, there are important risks that are excluded in this coverage, often including flood, wind, earthquake, and various types of losses that can affect motor vehicles and livestock. Other types of homeowner's coverage on the market today include *basic coverage* (HO-1), which covers only certain specifically named perils, and *broad coverage* (HO-2), which covers a wider list of threats.

Any homeowner's policy will cover the basic structure of the home up to a certain dollar amount or, if specified in the policy, its actual replacement cost; any unattached structures such as garages or swimming pools; personal property (even if the loss happens away from the home); and sometimes the additional living expenses that are incurred when a damaged home cannot be used pending repairs. A renter can get a *tenant's form* policy (HO-4) that covers only personal property and loss of use, and a condominium owner would get another form (HO-6) that protects the owner's individual unit only but excludes common areas such as hallways, which are covered under the condominium association's policy.

As is true of liability coverage, many policies exclude coverage for property owned by non-related roomers, tenants, or boarders; it is easy to see where an unmarried domestic partner could fit that legal description. In many cases, it will be necessary either to get a written acknowledgment that coverage is extended to both partners or to have separate policies.

Some high-value personal items such as jewelry, artwork, furs, and so forth, are excluded or are provided only minimal coverage under standard homeowner's policies. To protect these items adequately one must usually buy a separate "floater" policy that lists the specific asset being protected as well as an appraised value. You can record your homeowner's and automobile coverage on the worksheet that follows; it is also reproduced in the Appendix.

Insurance Summary

Name:

Part 4: Homeowner's

	Policy 1	Policy 2	Policy 3
Insurance Company			
Policy Number			
Insured Property			
Annual Premium			
Policy Type	HO-	HO-	HO-
Policy Limit—Dwelling			
Policy Limit—Contents			
Policy Limit—Liability			
Automatic Inflation Adjustment			
Cost to Replace Dwelling			
Market Value of Dwelling (except land)			
Replacement Cost Coverage			
Deductible			
Required Co-Insurance Percentage			

Part 5: Automobile

	Policy 1	Policy 2	Policy 3
Insurance Company			
Policy Number			
Insured Vehicle			
Annual Premium			
Principal Driver	HO-	HO-	HO-
Other Drivers			
Liability Limits—Bodily Injury (per person)			
Liability Limits—Bodily Injury (per accident)			
Liability Limits—Property Damage			
Collision Coverage? (if yes, deductible)			
Comprehensive Coverage?(if yes, deductible)			
Medical Payments			
Uninsured Motorist Coverage			

12

A Special Look at Trusts

The subject of trusts has come up many times in this book. Trusts are important in writing wills, protecting life insurance and other assets from estate taxes, safeguarding the assets of minors and incapacitated adults, and providing money management and other vital services on behalf of unskilled family members. Trusts are one of the most important devices we have to ensure that our money benefits the people we choose in the manner we choose. Unfortunately, trusts also scare most people, so much so that they are used less often than they should be.

A trust is essentially a business arrangement between two parties, not unlike a partnership or an *agency* (when one person represents the interests of another). As with those other business arrangements, the basic structure stays more or less the same, but the details can vary almost infinitely: Your trust can be nearly anything you want it to be.

Your attorney and other advisors can handle the details of establishing trusts for you. Your job is to understand how a trust works so that it can help you achieve your financial planning goals.

Structure of a Trust

The parties to a trust include the *grantor,* sometimes called the *settlor,* who creates the trust, and the *trustee,* sometimes called the *fiduciary,* who manages the trust in accordance with the wishes of the grantor. A trust also must have at least one *beneficiary.* The beneficiary is the person whose interests are to be served and protected under the trust. The beneficiary is not a party to the trust agreement, also called the *trust instrument,* and has no ability to change the terms of the agreement, unless of course the beneficiary is also either the grantor or the fiduciary. Any individual can play multiple roles in this process (grantor-trustee, grantor-beneficiary, beneficiary-trustee), but a trust cannot exist where the same person is the sole grantor, beneficiary, *and* fiduciary. (This last combination is outright ownership.)

Another prerequisite to have a trust is some *corpus*—that is, property that is subject to the trust agreement. Not infrequently, an individual establishes a trust that is not expected to have substantial assets until much later. For example, many people establish a trust during their lifetime to spell out how certain assets are to be distributed at death. Those people simply have their wills "pour over" assets from the estate into this trust, and then the trust governs the property. They do this because, if the distribution terms were put into the will itself, those terms would become public knowledge under the probate proceedings; the use of a pour-over trust arrangement maintains privacy. To make the trust valid until the substantial funding occurs, a nominal amount, like $10, is placed into the trust at the outset to serve as the corpus.

Here is what a very simple trust agreement might look like. The grantor is Jan, a parent; the trustee is Dick; and the beneficiary is Sally, Jan's daughter.

1. This is a trust agreement between Jan (the "Grantor") and Dick (the "Trustee") establishing "The Jan Family Trust of 1994."

2. Jan hereby transfers to Dick certain property consisting of publicly traded securities as further described on Schedule A. These securities shall constitute the initial corpus of the Jan Family Trust of 1994. Jan reserves the right to convey, at future dates and in such amounts as she deems desirable, additional property consisting of cash or publicly traded securities. Such cash or property shall be added to the trust corpus.

3. Dick agrees that he shall manage and conserve the trust property for the benefit of Jan's daughter Sally, born 12/11/76; that he will collect all income, manage all trust investments, and perform all legal and administrative functions ordinarily required of a trustee.

4. Dick shall pay all trust income to Sally or her legal guardian at least annually. At his discretion, Dick may make payments for Sally's benefit directly to schools, doctors, hospitals, or other providers of goods and services.

5. Any gains resulting from appreciation of capital shall be added to trust corpus and disposed of in accordance with Paragraph 6.

6. Sally shall receive half the trust corpus at her 25th birthday and the remainder of the trust corpus at her 30th birthday, free of trust.

7. If Sally should die at any time prior to her 30th birthday, she may by valid will referring specifically to this power of appointment, appoint the trust corpus to another individual (other than Jan, Jan's estate, Jan's creditors, or the creditors of Jan's estate). In the event she fails to

exercise this power of appointment, upon Sally's death the entire trust corpus shall be payable to Sally's heirs according to the laws governing intestate succession in the state of New York.

8. Dick shall have the broadest possible powers to manage the trust, including the power to hire attorneys, accountants, investment counsel, or such other professionals as he deems desirable.

9. This agreement shall be irrevocable.

10. Sally shall have no right to pledge, assign, or otherwise dispose of any property subject to this agreement nor to her rights granted under this agreement.

11. This agreement shall be interpreted and administered in accordance with the laws of the state of New York.

Signed this <u>Third</u> day of <u>   March,</u> 1994.

_____   _____

Jan   **Dick**

THE JAN FAMILY TRUST OF 1994
SCHEDULE A
PROPERTY TRANSFERRED TO TRUST ON MARCH 3, 1994

Security	**# Shares**	**Fair Market Val., 3/2/94**
Bone-Dry Dog Food Co., Inc.	1,000	$82,000
All-Wet Cat Food	500	$18,000

This brief agreement, or one like it, is all that is needed to make a valid trust in many places. You should work with an attorney to ensure that the specific language required by your jurisdiction is included. Jan might create this trust in order to minimize future gift and estate taxes (by transferring the publicly traded stock to Sally before it further increases in value), or to protect funds from future creditors' claims in the event Jan's financial fortunes take a tumble.

Dick assumes the duties of fiduciary in return for compensation, which is limited in most cases by state law. Trustee fees vary widely.

Revocable versus Irrevocable Trusts

A trust may be revocable or irrevocable. An irrevocable trust can neither be cancelled nor changed by its maker once it has been implemented, while a revocable trust can be changed quite easily without having to draft another entire trust agreement.

Revocable trusts are often used by people who want to avoid probate proceedings for certain property, or who want someone else to manage the property but otherwise wish to retain ownership. In these trusts, the grantor is usually either the sole or one of several beneficiaries, and also may be a co-trustee (although, remember, there must be at least one other person involved as beneficiary or trustee). The revocable trust can substitute for provisions in an individual's will. Since the trust is so easily cancelled or changed, it is very well-suited for this purpose, and has the added advantage of privacy.

Revocable trusts can be extremely valuable in planning for unmarried couples. We can see why in the following case.

▪ CASE 1: A Quiet Estate Plan

Brad's family was angry and disappointed when he revealed that he was gay. His parents would call him occasionally and invite him for family gatherings but made it clear that Roy, his lover, was unwelcome, so Brad stayed away. Brad's brothers did not even call.

Brad had done very well in business and had a net worth of several million dollars. He worried that if he left the money to Roy in his will Roy would have to defend against a legal challenge from Brad's family. He did not want Roy to have to go through that. In fact, Brad was sure that Roy would walk away from his rightful inheritance rather than pursue a nasty confrontation.

Brad's accountant suggested a revocable trust. Brad immediately called his lawyer and told him to draft a trust that would do the following:

1. Make Brad and Roy co-trustees. Now Roy would know that Brad had provided for him. Having Roy be co-trustee also meant Roy could legally handle everything if Brad became ill.

2. Provide that while Brad was alive, trust property (including income) could be distributed only to Brad. Brad's accountant advised him that this simplified the tax reporting and also avoided some potential estate-tax problems.

3. Make a gift of $50,000 to each of Brad's parents who are alive at Brad's death.

4. Pay off the mortgages on Brad's primary and vacation home and then give the properties, free and clear, to Roy.

5. Keep the remainder of Brad's property in trust for the balance of Roy's life. Roy would receive all income from the trust and as much trust principal as the trustee believed he required. The trustee after Brad's death would be the bank at which Brad did business.

6. At Roy's death, any property remaining in the trust would be divided and distributed to Brad's nieces and nephews once they reach adulthood. Brad deliberately avoided making any gift out of the trust to his brothers, with whom he was not on good terms.

When the trust was ready, Brad reregistered his bank and brokerage accounts to reflect the trust's ownership. He also changed his will to "pour over" any probate assets to the trust.

To reduce the chance of a successful challenge to the arrangement, Brad followed the same witnessing and other formalities in signing the trust document as would have been required for a will. At Brad's death nobody in his family even realized that his property had been placed in trust, and no challenge was initiated.

Irrevocable trusts are valuable for reducing estate taxes, since with few exceptions property that goes to an irrevocable trust can be excluded from the taxable estate of the transferor. The initial transfer to the trust may trigger gift tax, but judicious use of the annual exclusion and the unified credit can minimize out-of-pocket costs. As we saw in Chapter Ten, even a transfer that triggers payment of gift tax can be a smart financial move, since the overall transfer-tax burden is lower than estate taxes.

Of course, for unmarried couples an irrevocable trust has the major disadvantage of being inflexible in the event of a breakup or other subsequent event. A well-designed trust will avoid problems by providing for alternative disposition in the event a couple breaks up.

How Income Tax Is Applied to Trusts

Trusts are separate entities for income tax purposes and must have their own taxpayer identification number (obtained by filing Form SS-4 with the IRS). The trust may or may not be subject to income tax separately.

If the trust is a *grantor* trust, the trust property is treated (for income tax purposes) as if it were still owned by the grantor; the grantor reports all income or loss on his or her own tax return. Revocable trusts are always grantor trusts; other trusts may or may not be grantor trusts. The rules determining grantor trust status are fairly complex and are set forth in the Internal Revenue Code.*

If a trust is not a grantor trust, it generally must file Form 1041 and report its own income. Income that is distributed by the trust to the beneficiaries is deducted by the trust (the "distribution deduction") and is taxed directly to those beneficiaries. Only income which is retained by the trust, as well as taxable gain attributable to corpus (generally, capital gains) are taxed at the trust level.

A trust can be either *simple* or *complex.* Simple trusts are required to distribute all their income every year, in which case all income taxes are paid by the beneficiaries. Complex trusts have the authority to accumulate income and carry it from one year to the next. Either type may be used depending upon the objectives of the trust grantor. For example, a grantor may wish beneficiaries to receive a steady income flow and may choose a simple trust, or may prefer that the trust retain income until it is needed for some particular purpose.

The determination of taxable income for a trust is too complicated to cover here. Generally, one price of using a trust is a fee for professional help in preparing tax returns. When a trustee is a bank or other institution, tax preparation often is included in the trustee's fee.

Testamentary Trusts

Some trusts are established after the grantor's death. These are *testamentary trusts,* and their terms are spelled out in the individual's will.

* I.R.C. Secs. 671–679.

Testamentary trusts usually have the same terms that an individual might have used in a revocable or irrevocable trust established during life, except that of course the grantor will have no role in the trust as beneficiary.

In some cases an individual will want to bequeath assets for the benefit of a domestic partner during the partner's lifetime, and thereafter to benefit the grantor's children or other relatives. Often it is impossible to know when the will or trust is being written whether or not those "remainder" beneficiaries (who take the remainder of the trust after the lifetime beneficiary, in this case the domestic partner) are best treated equally. Giving the life beneficiary a "special power of appointment" can be a big help. The next case illustrates.

▲ CASE 2: Who Gets What

Rick and Ella had two children but chose not to get married. Rick had a good job as a technical illustrator at an aerospace concern and they lived comfortably with daughters Kimberly, four and Andrea, two, before Rick was killed in a boating accident.

Rick's brother was an attorney who had helped him with his estate planning. Rick carried $900,000 in life insurance. When Kimberly was born he had placed his private $500,000 policy in an irrevocable trust, naming Ella as the life beneficiary and the girls as remainder beneficiaries. The remaining $400,000 was employer-sponsored insurance for which Rick named Ella as beneficiary.

No estate taxes were due at Rick's death because his unified credit offset the $400,000 of employer-sponsored insurance that remained in his estate. Once the girls were in school, Ella returned to her career as a marketing analyst, and except for major purchases and the kids' education, the life insurance money remained largely untouched.

Shortly after she turned eighteen Andrea developed severe schizophrenia and had to be institutionalized. The costs exceeded $60,000 a year, but because Andrea was legally an adult and had no assets, Medicaid paid the bills.

Ella changed her will to exercise a special power of appointment over Rick's insurance trust. Kimberly was made the sole beneficiary in the event of Ella's death, to avoid having assets go to Andrea and cause immediate termination of her Medicaid coverage.

A power of appointment needs to be carefully drafted. Too broad a power can cause the trust property to be included in the power holder's estate. A touchy situation also can arise when the power holder has closer ties to some beneficiaries than to others (e.g., when the grantor has two children, one of which is with the power holder and the other by a prior relationship). In these cases, alternate arrangements may have to be made, perhaps even including two separate trusts.

Charity and More

A special kind of trust which includes a qualified charity as a beneficiary can provide unusual financial planning opportunities—even if charitable giving is not one of your financial objectives.

These kinds of trusts are called *split interest trusts* because the economic benefits are split between a charity and one or more noncharitable beneficiaries, such as you or your domestic partner. There are two basic kinds of split interest trusts. A *charitable lead trust* gives the charity the right to receive annual payments from the trust for a period of time known as the *term,* after which the property goes to the non-charitable beneficiaries. A *charitable remainder trust* does the opposite, making payments during the term to non-charitable beneficiaries, after which the trust property goes to the charity. The term payments may be either a fixed dollar amount ("annuity trusts") or a fixed percentage of the trust's value ("unitrusts").

A charitable lead trust is usually used when charitable giving is a major financial objective. For this reason, it is outside the scope of this book. A charitable remainder trust, however, has important advantages that often make it worthwhile regardless of charitable intent. The next case provides an example.

♣ CASE 3: Safe Haven

Lydia was wealthy, thanks to a large inheritance of MegaBrand Corporation stock. The stock had been Lydia's grandmother's, and she in turn had inherited it from *her* father, who founded a company that was acquired by MegaBrand. Lydia, forty-two, was interested in environmental work, as was her domestic partner Alice, who was thirty-five. Lydia wanted to quit her marketing job to devote herself to environmental causes.

To live on her portfolio, however, Lydia felt she had to make some changes. She did not want MegaBrand to be the dominant holding because if anything happened to that company Lydia's financial future would be in jeopardy. Also, MegaBrand paid a very small dividend, and Lydia wanted at least $180,000 a year to live on. Her investment advisor suggested a portfolio that would be 50% bonds (to provide interest income to live on), 30% U.S. growth stocks, and 20% foreign stocks. The bonds would pay 6% interest after taxes; the stocks were expected to grow in value by 12% per year.

Lydia got some disappointing news, however, when she met with her accountant to discuss the proposed change. The inherited stock had virtually no cost basis, so taxes would consume about one third of the sales proceeds. Her accountant prepared this projection:

MegaBrand Sale	$6,000,000	
Less Taxes	<2,000,000>	
Amount to Invest	$4,000,000	
Bonds 50%	$2,000,000	$120,000 income
U.S. Stocks (30%)	$1,200,000	12% annual growth
Foreign Stocks (20%)	$ 800,000	12% annual growth
Total Portfolio	$4,000,000	

Because of the large capital gains tax, Lydia saw, she would not have sufficient income to live on unless she diverted some money out of stocks. But if she diverted money out of stocks, she felt she would not have sufficient growth potential to hedge against future inflation. Lydia felt trapped and frustrated.

Her accountant suggested that Lydia consider establishing a charitable remainder unitrust instead. The big advantage of a charitable trust, the accountant pointed out, is that it does not pay capital gains tax. The $6 million of Lydia's MegaBrand stock could be sold and the entire proceeds put to work to provide an income stream for her and Alice. Since Lydia did not need 5% of the trust's value ($300,000) every year, the trust was written to limit the distributions to the amount of income earned by the trust; this limited the payout to $180,000 (6% interest earned on the $3 million that would be invested in bonds).

Now Lydia had ample cash for her current needs and a $3 million diversified portfolio invested for future growth, rather than $2 million. Because Lydia was very confident in her relationship with Alice, she wrote the trust to provide income to Alice after Lydia's death; only when both of them were deceased would the trust corpus go to charity. Selecting the charitable recipient was easy. Lydia picked the environmental group that was her new employer.

Sometimes a charitable remainder trust is combined with an irrevocable life insurance trust in a *wealth replacement* trust arrangement. Basically, some of the income from the charitable trust is used to finance the purchase of life insurance, which compensates the grantor's family for the fact that the charitable trust corpus ultimately goes to the charity.

Often people live with unwise and undiversified investments because they do not want to incur the capital gains tax that results from selling and reinvesting. Most of these situations are good candidates for charitable remainder trusts, which also provide a convenient vehicle to provide a lifetime of income to a domestic partner.

There are alternatives to trusts that have been discussed elsewhere in this book. These include joint ownership, agency, and partnerships. Don't be paralyzed by confusion over which one to use; focus instead on clearly defining your goals. Then find an expert who understands what you want to do and has the skill to help you do it.

13

A Changing Legal Landscape

The forces that change our society move in fits and starts, the way an earthquake or volcano abruptly rearranges the landscape.

Look at all that has happened within the lifetime of even the youngest Baby Boomers: passage of the civil rights protections for racial and other minorities; the emergence of women in the labor market; legalization of abortion; the decline of the inner city.

So it is with unmarried domestic partners. Just a few decades ago most of these relationships met with intolerance or ostracism; today they are widely accepted. The easy gains, however, have been made. Now comes the hard part.

On May 5, 1993, the Hawaii Supreme Court ruled that the state's ban on homosexual marriages is "presumed to be unconstitutional" unless the state can find compelling reasons to justify it. More litigation will follow, and it remains to be seen whether the ruling will, as many gay-rights advocates hope, open the door for same-sex marriages.

Assuming Hawaii or some other state *does* someday permit same-sex marriages, what will be the impact elsewhere? Until now, states have generally recognized marriages performed in other jurisdictions; this is the basis of an entire wedding-chapel industry in Nevada. Other states' marriages are respected even when the couple could not legally have been married locally, such as in cases when one individual is underage according to local law. This tradition of accommodation notwithstanding, if Hawaii or any other state begins formalizing same-sex marriages, we can expect attempts in other jurisdictions to deny recognition to those unions.

Denying home-state recognition of same-sex marriages would pose an interesting dilemma for the IRS. Much of the federal tax law revolves around the individual's marital status. What if one state (where the ceremony was conducted) recognizes a marriage, but the individual's state of residence does not? We will have to wait for courts and legislatures, including a very reluctant Congress, to answer these questions.

Public policy on unconventional relationships can be set in many ways. For example, while the United States debated the issue of gays in the military during and after the 1992 presidential campaign, the courts in Canada were well on their way toward resolving the same question for that country. In August 1992 the Ontario Court of Appeals ruled unanimously that, although protection for homosexuals was not explicitly provided in that country's Human Rights Act, such protection must be "read in" to the law; otherwise the statute would conflict with the Canadian Charter of Rights and Freedoms. The court wrote:

> The social context which must be considered includes the pain and humiliation undergone by homosexuals by reason of prejudice towards them. It also includes the enlightened evolution of human rights social and legislative policy in Canada, since the end of the Second World War, both provincially and federally. The failure to provide an avenue for redress for prejudicial treatment of homosexual members of society, and the possible inference from the omission [of language in the Human Rights Act explicitly protecting homosexuals] that such treatment is acceptable, create the effect of discrimination offending s.15(1) of the Charter. . . . The denial to homosexual persons of the equal protection and equal benefit of the law without discrimination by reason of the denial to them of access to the remedial provi-

sions of the Canadian Human Rights Act must be held to be unjustified in a free and democratic society.*

The Ontario court's ruling had national impact north of the border, giving homosexuals across Canada the right to bring action against the military and other government institutions for discrimination. In October 1992, a lower court followed the appeal court's ruling and overturned the military's policy barring homosexuals from promotion, training, and other career opportunities.†

Is the Canadian situation very different from ours? It seems to depend on your point of view. The section of the Canadian Charter of Rights and Freedoms on which the Ontario court ruling was based simply says:

> Every individual is equal before and under the law and has the right to the equal protection and equal benefit of the law without discrimination and, in particular, without discrimination based on race, national or ethnic origin, colour, religion, sex, age or mental or physical disability.**

The analogous section of the U.S. Constitution is in the Fourteenth Amendment, particularly the "equal protection clause" which is the last sentence. The Fourteenth Amendment reads:

> All persons born or naturalized in the United States, and subject to the jurisdiction thereof, are citizens of the United States and of the State wherein they reside. No State shall make or enforce any law which shall abridge the privileges or immunities of citizens of the United States; nor shall any State deprive any person of life, liberty, or property, without

---

* *Haig* v. *Canada (Minister of Justice),* Ontario Court of Appeals, O.J. No. 1609, August 6, 1992.
† *Douglas* v. *Canada,* F.C.J. No. 948, Federal Court of Canada—Trial Division, October 27, 1992.
** Canadian Charter of Rights and Freedoms, Sec. 15(1).

due process of law; nor deny to any person within its jurisdiction the equal protection of the laws.

Both the Canadian and U.S. constitutions mention "equal protection"; Canada also refers to "equal benefit" of the law. Even in
Canada this has not, so far, led to recognized same-sex marriages,
although the Canadian courts say these constitutional provisions
mean legalized, government-implemented discrimination is not allowed.

Here in the States, the law has in essence taken the position
that everyone, gay or straight, has an equal opportunity to get married (to someone of the opposite sex, of course), and therefore
there is no discrimination. Of course, many homosexuals would
argue that, for them, this is only an opportunity to choose an unhappy life followed by a messy divorce.

Our society is deeply divided over the rights of unmarried couples, particularly homosexuals. As with so many other areas that fall
within the realm of "privacy," we debate the state's need and its
power to reward certain types of conduct and sanction others.

If we could take some of the moralizing and emotion out of the
argument we might want to ask ourselves the following questions:

✓ Do we want our laws to encourage people to enter into
long-term commitments to each other, to rely on each
other for emotional and material support, and to protect
the rights of people who enter into such relationships in
good faith?

✓ Is our society better off when two people can arrange a
division of labor that is best suited to their skills, each
knowing that the law values his or her contribution and
will ensure an equitable division of resources when the
couple is parted, by death or otherwise?

✓ Should our government, founded on a respect for
pluralism, proscribe certain partners as "inappropriate"

for the minority who would choose them, merely because
that choice would offend the moral or religious
sensibilities of others?

For most of us, the "pursuit of happiness" mentioned in our
Declaration of Independence means the pursuit of love and affection. Our law should not demand that people make do without that
affection, nor should it penalize people for taking it wherever they
choose to take it. Denying legal and economic recognition to same-
sex domestic partners devalues these relationships in a way that,
from objective tax, economic, and legal viewpoints, is unjustified.

A great deal of inequity could be wiped out immediately if
federal law allowed members of unmarried couples to designate
("elect," in tax parlance) a "spouse" for federal tax purposes. Because many state laws automatically follow federal treatment,
designating a spouse would resolve many tax problems at the state
tax level as well. Taxpayers already have all sorts of discretion to
make elections under our tax code; there are well-established procedures administered by the IRS for making and revoking these
elections. Congress could put the language in the next tax bill. It
might read:

SECTION 154: SPOUSAL ELECTION
FOR DOMESTIC PARTNERS

a) For purposes of all taxes imposed under Chapters 1, 11,
12, 13, and 14 [the federal income, gift, estate, and genera-
tion-skipping transfer taxes], the term *spouse* shall mean:

1) The individual to whom the taxpayer is legally married under local law.
2) If the taxpayer is not legally married under local law,
the individual with respect to whom taxpayer has made
the election described in subsection b).

b) ELECTION TO TREAT ANOTHER INDIVIDUAL AS A SPOUSE—A taxpayer who is not legally married under local law may elect to treat another individual as a spouse for purposes of all taxes imposed by Chapters 1, 11, 12, 13, and 14. Such election shall:

1) Be filed prior to the first day of the tax year in which it is to take effect.

2) Remain in effect until the first day of the tax year commencing after the year in which the election is revoked. If a taxpayer files an election with respect to more than one individual, other than in accordance with the terms for revoking a prior election and filing a new election, only the first election shall be effective.

3) Be effective only if a reciprocal election has been filed by the individual designated as the taxpayer's spouse, in which the designated spouse has so designated the taxpayer.

4) Be effective only if the taxpayer and the designated spouse have, as the principal residence of each of them, the same dwelling unit.

5) Not be effective if there is a relationship between the taxpayer and the designated spouse by blood, adoption, or marriage which would prevent their becoming legally married under local law. Such relationship shall include but not be limited to mother, father, brother, sister, aunt, uncle, grandmother, and grandfather. The fact that taxpayer and the designated spouse are of the same gender shall not, by itself, constitute a relationship that prevents their becoming legally married.

6) Be made and revoked in accordance with procedures to be prescribed by the Commissioner.

c) LIMITATION—If a taxpayer has revoked an election made under this section, taxpayer shall be ineligible to make another such election for four (4) years commencing on the first day of the tax year following revocation.

d) AUTOMATIC TERMINATION—An election under this section shall terminate on the last day of the tax year preceding a year in which the taxpayer becomes legally married under local law.

That should do it—a clear, simple procedure by which a taxpayer could designate an individual to be a spouse for tax purposes even if they remain unmarried for other purposes. I have deliberately not limited the language to same-sex couples, since heterosexual couples may need to avail themselves of the same rules. This language would eliminate the tax system's bias toward traditional marriages and would, instead, respect any legitimate domestic partnership on the same terms. It would not permit anything like a "group marriage" or similar relationship beyond the two-individual couple. The legislation would also prevent relatives or non-cohabiting friends from "marrying" each other for tax purposes, which they might otherwise do to file joint income tax returns, to take advantage of the unlimited gift and estate tax marital deduction, or for other reasons.

As tax law goes, this is a very straightforward section. I hope Congress someday passes something like it. But if you want my professional advice, don't hold your breath.

Today's law certainly puts unmarried couples at a financial disadvantage. Societal pressures add to the strain. But we have seen in this book that most of the financial arrangements an unmarried couple might want to make can, in fact, be accomplished with good planning.

Now it is your turn. Whatever your reason for not making the legal commitment of marriage, you can achieve many of the same results if you want to. Be honest with yourself and with each other about what you have and what you want. Then you will be ready to plan and build your future.

Appendix

Key Facts List

Name:

Date Prepared:

Personal Data:

Birth Date: _____

Social Security Number: _____

Location of Principal Home: _____

Location of Other Homes: _____

Citizen of: _____

Domestic Partner

Name: _____

Birth Date: _____

Social Security Number: _____

Location of Principal Home: _____

Location of Other Homes: _____

Citizen of: _____

Child #1

Name: _____

Birth Date: _____

Social Security Number: _____

Custodial Parent: _____

Address & Phone: _____

Is Child Married ? (Y/N): _____

Spouse's Name: _____

Location of Principal Home: _____

Location of Other Homes: _____

Citizen of: _____

Child's Dependents: _____

_____

_____

Child #2

Name: _____

Birth Date: _____

Social Security Number: _____

Custodial Parent: _____

Address & Phone: _____

Is Child Married ? (Y/N): _____

Spouse's Name: _____

Location of Principal Home: _____

Location of Other Homes: _____

Citizen of: _____

Child's Dependents: _____

_____

_____

Child #3

Name: _____

Birth Date: _____

Social Security Number: _____

Custodial Parent: _____

Address & Phone: _____

Is Child Married ? (Y/N): _____

Spouse's Name: _____

Location of Principal Home: _____

Location of Other Homes: _____

Citizen of: _____

Child's Dependents: _____

_____

_____

Key Facts List

Financial Advisors

Attorney (business):

Firm Name: _____
Street Address: _____
City, State, ZIP: _____
Telephone: _____

Attorney (personal):

Firm Name: _____
Street Address: _____
City, State, ZIP: _____
Telephone: _____

Accountant (business):

Firm Name: _____
Street Address: _____
City, State, ZIP: _____
Telephone: _____

Accountant (personal):

Firm Name: _____
Street Address: _____
City, State, ZIP: _____
Telephone: _____

Life Insurance Agent:

Company: _____
Street Address: _____
City, State, ZIP: _____
Telephone: _____

Employer:

Firm Name: _____
Street Address: _____
City, State, ZIP: _____
Telephone: _____

Property/Casualty Agent:

Company: _____
Street Address: _____
City, State, ZIP: _____
Telephone: _____

Stockbroker:

Firm Name: _____
Street Address: _____
City, State, ZIP: _____
Telephone: _____

Financial Planner:

Firm Name: _____
Street Address: _____
City, State, ZIP: _____
Telephone: _____

Banker (business):

Firm Name: _____
Street Address: _____
City, State, ZIP: _____
Telephone: _____

Banker (personal):

Firm Name: _____
Street Address: _____
City, State, ZIP: _____
Telephone: _____

Physician:

Firm/Hospital: _____
Street Address: _____
City, State, ZIP: _____
Telephone: _____

Key Facts List

Document Locator

Document	Doc. Date	Location	Notes
Contracts			
Marital/Premarital/Living			
Business Buy/Sell			
Employment			
Partnership			
Other			
Property Records			
Bank Statements			
Brokerage Statements			
Employee Benefit Statements			
Stock Certificates			
Bonds, Promissory Notes			
Automobile Title			
Boat Title			
Other Personal Property Title			
Personal Property Inventory			
Primary Residence Closing Papers			
Vacation Home Closing Papers			
Other Real Estate Closing Papers			
Cemetery Plot Title			
List of Real Estate Improvements			
Mortgages			
Personal Records			
Birth Certificate			
Baptismal Records			
Divorce Papers			
Marriage License			
Medical Records			
Passport			
Immigration/Naturalization Papers			
Social Security Card			
Income Tax Returns			
Gift Tax Returns			
Tax Records			
Income Tax Returns			
Gift Tax Returns			
Receipts, Cancelled Checks, etc.			
Insurance Records			
Life Insurance Policies			
Health Insurance Policies			
Disability Insurance Policies			
Homeowner's Policies			
Other Policies			
Estate Planning			
Will			
Trust Agreements			
Living Will			
Durable Power of Attorney			
Health-Care Power of Attorney			
Funeral Instructions			

Net Worth Statement

Name: _____   **Assets:** _____   **Date:** _____

	Current Value	Tax Cost (A)	Potential Tax on Sale (B)	Net Value
Liquid				
Cash (checking, savings accounts)				
Short-term investments				
Treasury bills				
Savings certificates				
Money market funds				
Cash value of life insurance				
Total Liquid Assets				
Investment				
Notes receivable				
Publicly traded stocks				
Taxable bonds				
Tax-exempt bonds				
Investment real estate				
Non-marketable securities				
Retirement funds				
Other				
Total Investment Assets				
Personal				
Principal residence				
Vacation property				
Art, antiques				
Furnishings				
Vehicles				
Boats				
Other				
Total Personal Assets				
Total Assets				

NOTES:

(A): Tax cost, or basis, is the amount you are deemed to have invested in the asset for tax purposes. The greater the basis, the less the potential tax if you decide to sell the asset.

(B): Potential tax on sale is the estimated tax you would pay if you sold the asset. You compute this by subtracting the tax cost from the market value of the asset, then multiplying by the tax rate. (For many taxpayers, asset sales are likely to be taxed at more favorable capital gains rates.) Your true net worth is the market value of your assets less this accrued tax. Note that under present law, however, no capital gains tax would be due on assets you bequeath to others when you die, because the assets receive a new tax basis equal to the fair market value at your death (a "stepped-up basis").

Net Worth Statement

Liabilities

	Current Value	Net Value
Short Term		
(Due in Less Than 2 Years)		
Credit Card debt	_____	_____
Auto, boat, etc. loans	_____	_____
Installment loans	_____	_____
Education loans	_____	_____
Borrowings on life insurance	_____	_____
Brokerage margin accounts	_____	_____
Other debt	_____	_____
Total Short-Term Liabilities	_____	_____
Long Term		
(Due in More Than 2 Years)		
Loans to purchase personal assets	_____	_____
Loan to acquire business	_____	_____
Mortgages	_____	_____
Total Long-Term Liabilities	_____	_____
Total Liabilities	_____	_____
Total Net Worth	_____	_____

Household Budget

Income	Current Year	Next Year (est.)
Your Salary		
Your Bonus		
Domestic Partner Salary (Opt.)		
Domestic Partner Bonus (Opt.)		
Other Compensation		
Dividends		
Interest		
Capital Gains		
Other		
Other		
Total Income		

Expenses	Current Year	Next Year (est.)
Fixed Expenses		
Taxes & Withholding		
Groceries		
Mortgage		
Other Loans & Credit Cards		
Property Tax		
Utilities		
Home Maintenance		
Clothing & Dry Cleaning		
Uninsured Medical & Dental		
Child Care		
Car Loans		
Gasoline & Oil		
Car Repairs & Maintenance		
Insurance: Life, Home, Car		
Tuition		
Total Fixed Expenses		
Variable Expenses		
Major Purchases		
Restaurants		
Entertainment		
Telephone		
Vacation		
Books, CDs, Magazines		
Fitness		
Personal Grooming		
Gifts		
Charitable Donations		
Other		
Total Variable Expenses		
Total Expenses		
SURPLUS OR SHORT FALL		

Gifts to Domestic Partner (Balance Sheet Method)

Date:

NOTE: Some unmarried couples may want to share in the overall increase in wealth that they accumulate during their relationship, as married couples do under the law. This work-sheet allows you and your domestic partner to devise a program of annual gifts that measure and then equalize the change in your financial position. You can, of course, modify this program any way you wish, such as by removing a partner's business assets from the calculation.

	Beginning of Year			End of Year		
Assets	Partner #1	Partner #2	Total Value	Partner #1	Partner #2	Total Value
Liquid Assets	____	____	____	____	____	____
Investment Assets	____	____	____	____	____	____
Personal Assets	____	____	____	____	____	____
Total Assets	____	____	____	____	____	____
Liabilities	Partner #1	Partner #2	Difference			
Short-Term Debt	____	____	____			
Long-Term Debt	____	____	____			
Total Liabilities	____	____	____			
Total Net Worth	____	____	____			
NET WORTH—END OF YEAR	____					
NET WORTH—BEGINNING OF YEAR	____					
INCREASE (DECREASE)	____					
COMPENSATING GIFT	____ 50% of Difference					
(from partner with greater increase)	____					

Estate Planning Questionnaire

NOTE: Your attorney can use the information you compile in this section as a guide in preparing your will and other estate planning documents. In the author's opinion, individuals without specific training or education in this complex area of the law should not draft their own documents. However, if you do, you should consider having them reviewed by a competent attorney.

In addition to this questionnaire, you should provide your attorney with information on your financial resources compiled on the worksheets elsewhere in this book, as needed.

Part 1: Beneficiaries

	Name & Date of Birth	Address	Social Security #
Your Domestic Partner:	_____	_____	_____
		_____	
Your Children:	_____	_____	_____
(Identify even if you plan no bequest)		_____	
	_____	_____	_____
		_____	
	_____	_____	_____
		_____	
Your Grandchildren:	_____	_____	_____
(Identify even if you plan no bequest) (Identify each grandchild's parent)		_____	
	_____	_____	_____
		_____	
	_____	_____	_____
		_____	
	_____	_____	_____
		_____	
Other Beneficiaries:	_____	_____	_____
		_____	
	_____	_____	_____
		_____	
	_____	_____	_____
		_____	

Estate Planning Questionnaire

Part 2: Estate Administration

Identify the individuals or firms who will play a role in managing the affairs of your estate.

	Name	Address	Telephone Number
Executor (personal representative)			
Co-Executor			
Alternate Executor			
Trustee			
Co-Trustee			
Alternate Trustee			
Guardian(s) for Minor Children			
Alternate Guardian(s)			
Investment Manager			
Accountant			
Attorney			

Estate Planning Questionnaire

Part 3: Disposition of Assets

1. What items of property would you wish to leave to specific individuals?

Item   **Recipient**   **Estimated Value**

2. What amounts of money would you wish to leave to specific individuals?

Amount   **Recipient**

3. To whom should the remainder of your estate be distributed?

Percentage   **Recipient**

4. Do you wish to place a certain portion of your estate in trust to benefit one individual

   (e.g., your domestic partner) during his/her lifetime and others thereafter?

   If so, indicate below.

Amount or Percentage   **Life Recipient**

                                 Remaindermen
                                 (Beneficiaries after life recipient's death)

5. Should children receive property at legal adulthood, or at a later age? If you prefer to defer distributions until later ages, indicate age and percentage or amount to be distributed.

Amount or Percentage   **Age at Distribution**

6. If any beneficiaries have special educational, medical or financial needs, indicate below.

Estate Planning Questionnaire

Part 4: Other Estate Planning Documents

1. Are you the creator or beneficiary of any trusts? If so, describe.

2. Do you wish to give another individual powers to manage your financial affairs in the event you become disabled? If so, have you executed a durable power of attorney?

3. Do you wish to give another individual powers to make health-care decisions on your behalf in the event you are unable to do so? If yes, have you executed a health-care power of attorney?

4. Do you wish to provide a statement of your intent regarding the use of life-prolonging medical procedures in the event you are incapacitated and terminally ill? If yes, have you executed a living will?

Insurance Summary

Name:

Part 1: Life Insurance

	Policy 1	Policy 2	Policy 3
Insurance Company			
Policy Number			
Insured			
Year Issued			
Face Amount			
Current Death Benefit (if different from face amount)			
Current Surrender (Cash) Value			
Annual Premium			
Total Premiums Paid to Date			
Premium Expected to Be Paid Through Year _____ (see Note A)			
Policy Loans Outstanding			
Interest Rate on Policy Loans			
Policy Owner			
Primary Beneficiary(ies)			
Contingent Beneficiary(ies)			
Dividend Option (see Note B)			

NOTES:

(A): If premiums are expected to be paid for life, indicate "life." If a premium "vanish" is expected, indicate the last year cash premiums are expected to be due for each policy. Note that premium vanish years can differ from initial sales projections due to changes in insurance company charges and dividends.

(B): Typical dividend options are to be paid in cash, to reduce premiums, to purchase additional paid-up insurance (PUAs), or to be deposited in an interest-bearing account with the insurance company.

Life Insurance Requirements

Name:

Cash Required at Death

Funeral _____

Estate administration _____

Estate taxes _____

Emergency fund for family expenses _____

Current bills _____

Total _____

Cash Available at Death

Insurance proceeds _____

Death benefits of retirement programs _____

Liquid assets _____

Other

Total _____

Net Cash Available (or Required) at Death

_____

Assets Available for Mortgage and Children's Education

Mortgage outstanding _____

Education (see Note A) _____

Total _____

Assets Available for Mortgage and Children's Education

Investment assets _____

Personal assets convertible to cash _____

Other _____

Total _____

Net Assets Available (Required) for Mortgage and Education

_____

Survivor Living Expenses (Note B)

_____

Income Available for Survivor Living Expenses

Income from assets _____

Employment income of survivor(s) _____

Other _____

Total _____

Annual Income Excess (or Deficiency)

_____

Additional Insurance Required

Cash required at death _____

Mortgage and education _____

Living expenses _____

_____

NOTES:

(A): This is the amount which, if invested today, would grow to a sum sufficient to provide the desired contribution to children's educational expenses.

(B): This is the amount which, if invested today, would provide an income stream to surviving domestic partner, children, or other beneficiaries for the desired length of time.

Insurance Summary

Name:

Part 2: Disability

	Policy 1	Policy 2	Policy 3
Insurance Company	_____	_____	_____
Policy Number	_____	_____	_____
Insured	_____	_____	_____
Year Issued	_____	_____	_____
Annual Premium	_____	_____	_____
Monthly Benefit	_____	_____	_____
Definition of Disability (see Note A)	_____	_____	_____
Waiting (Elimination) Period	_____	_____	_____
Benefit Period (see Note B)	_____	_____	_____
Cost-of-Living Adjustment	_____	_____	_____
Guaranteed Renewable	_____	_____	_____
Partial Disability Coverage	_____	_____	_____
Residual Disability Coverage	_____	_____	_____
Retraining Benefits	_____	_____	_____

NOTES:

(A): Usual definitions of disability provide benefits when insured cannot perform duties of: 1) own occupation; 2) any occupation for which he/she is reasonably suited by training and experience; 3) any occupation; 4) some combination of above (e.g. #1 for first two years, #3 thereafter).

(B): Benefits under disability policies are payable until death, until age 65, or for a shorter period as provided under the policy.

Insurance Summary

Name:

Part 3: Medical

	Policy 1	Policy 2	Policy 3
Insured Person(s)	_____	_____	_____
Insurance Company	_____	_____	_____
HMO, PPO, or Other "Managed Care"?	_____	_____	_____
Group Policy/Program?	_____	_____	_____
Annual Premium	_____	_____	_____
Authorization Required for Emergency Treatment? (if yes, give telephone number)	_____	_____	_____
Authorization Required For Non-Emergency Treatment? (if yes, give telephone number)	_____	_____	_____
Major Medical (except HMOs):	_____	_____	_____
Annual Limit—Individual	_____	_____	_____
Annual Limit—Family	_____	_____	_____
Deductible—Individual	_____	_____	_____
Deductible—Family	_____	_____	_____
Lifetime Limit—Individual	_____	_____	_____
Lifetime Limit—Family	_____	_____	_____
Co-Payment Percentage	_____	_____	_____
Co-Payment Applies to First $$?	_____	_____	_____
Hospitalization (except HMOs):	_____	_____	_____
Daily Room Charge Covered	_____	_____	_____
Maximum Number of Days	_____	_____	_____
Maximum Other Expenses (except surgery)	_____	_____	_____
Maximum Surgical Expense	_____	_____	_____

Financial Goals Worksheet

Name:

Date:

Step 1: Identify and Classify Financial Objectives

For each of the following financial objectives, identify its importance to you (high, medium, low, none), and indicate whether achieving the objective is a short-term goal (within 2 years), medium-term (2–10 years), or long-term (more than 10 years).

Objective	Term	IMPORTANCE High	Medium	Low	None
Spending & Lifestyle					
Improve Present Standard of Living (spending)	____	____	____	____	____
Improve Future Standard of Living (spending)	____	____	____	____	____
Financial Independence at Age ___	____	____	____	____	____
Retirement at Age ___	____	____	____	____	____
New Home	____	____	____	____	____
Vacation Home	____	____	____	____	____
New Car/Truck	____	____	____	____	____
New Boat, Airplane, Other Vehicle	____	____	____	____	____
Extensive Travel	____	____	____	____	____
Weddings, Bar Mitzvah, Other Large Affair	____	____	____	____	____
Other	____	____	____	____	____
Dependent Support					
Own Education (college, grad school, trade school, etc.)	____	____	____	____	____
Children's Education	____	____	____	____	____
Support Elderly Parents	____	____	____	____	____
Support Domestic Partner	____	____	____	____	____
Gifts to Loved Ones	____	____	____	____	____
Gifts to Charity	____	____	____	____	____
Other	____	____	____	____	____
Saving & Investment					
Build Financial Cushion	____	____	____	____	____
Build Retirement Fund	____	____	____	____	____
Change Career	____	____	____	____	____
Start Business	____	____	____	____	____
Other	____	____	____	____	____

Financial Goals Worksheet

Step 2: Organize Goals by Time Horizon

In this section you should list the goals you established in Part 1. Put each goal in the appropriate time horizon and list them in order of priority, beginning with the most important.

	IMPORTANCE		
	High	Medium	Low
Short-Term Goals			
Medium-Term Goals			
Long-Term Goals			

Financial Goals Worksheet

Step 3: Compute Funds for Goals

NOTE: To complete these calculations you will need a financial calculator, a personal computer, or a hand-held calculator and separate tables of future and present values of $1 and future value of an annuity in advance (an "annuity due").

This worksheet allows you to compute the funding required to meet each financial goal under one of two methods: 1) A lump sum, invested today; 2) a series of periodic (annual) investments.

1. Financial Goal:	_____
2. Current Savings for Goal:	_____
3. Estimated Cost (current dollars):	_____
4. Number of Years to Reach Goal:	_____
5. Estimated Future Inflation:	_____
6. Estimated Aftertax Return on Investments:	_____

Computation of Lump-Sum Amount

Lump-Sum Required = (PV $1, at estimated aftertax
return on investments, for number of years to reach
goal)   _____

Future Cost of Goal = (Estimated cost in current dollars)
x (FV $1, at estimated future inflation rate, for number
of years to reach goal)   _____

Subtract Future Cost from Lump Sum. This is the
additional amount you should invest today to achieve the
specified goal.   ============

Computation of Required Annual Contribution

Future Value of Current Savings = (Current savings) x
(FV $1, at estimated aftertax return on investments, for
number of years to reach goal)   _____

Future Cost of Goal = (Estimated cost in current dollars)
x (FV $1, at estimated future inflation rate, for number
of years to reach goal)   _____

Amount to be Saved Through Annual Contributions =
(Future Cost - Future Value of Current Savings)   _____

Required Annual Contribution = (Amount to be saved) /
(FVA , at estimated aftertax return on investments, for
number of years to goal)   ============

Asset Allocation Worksheet

NOTE: This worksheet helps you allocate your investments among stocks, bonds and money market instruments in a way that is consistent with your investment goals and tolerance for risk. Use this form in conjunction with the Goal-Setting Worksheet to develop an asset allocation that meets your financial needs without accepting undue risk.

Part 1: Compute Your Real Rate of Return for Various Investments

To complete this section you must estimate your future combined federal and state income tax rate. Based on historical performance (considering inflation), each investment category has a pretax rate of return listed in Column A. In Column B, enter 1 minus your estimated tax rate. (For example, if your estimated rate is 33%, you would enter 1 − .33, or 67%.) Multiply the pretax return by your tax rate to find your estimated aftertax real rate of return for each investment, and enter the appropriate amounts in Column C.

	A Real Return Pretax	B Estimated Tax Rate	C Real Return Aftertax
Investment			
Treasury Bills	0.50%		
Bank Accounts, Money Market Funds	0.75%		
Long-Term Government Bonds	1.40%		
Long-Term Corporate Bonds	2.00%		
Common Stock	7.50%		

Asset Allocation Worksheet

Part 2: Define Your Risk Tolerance

Find the statement that best describes your willingness to accept investment risk.

Statement	Risk Tolerance
I seek maximum long-term growth of my capital. I do not care about receiving significant current payments of income, and I am willing to accept large fluctuations in the value of my investments.	Very High
I want significant long-term growth of my capital. However, I do not like extremely speculative investments and prefer to avoid excessive swings in portfolio value. Current income is a consideration, although secondary to achieving capital growth.	High
I want to achieve a balance between growth and income. Some portfolio swings, up to perhaps a 20% increase or decrease in total value over short periods, are acceptable; I am uncomfortable with larger swings. I am willing to sacrifice some long-term return to invest within these constraints.	Moderate
I want to achieve a reasonable rate of income from my portfolio. Capital growth is a secondary consideration, although it is nonetheless important to me. I do not wish to experience short-term fluctuations in portfolio value greater than about 15%.	Moderately Low
I want the value of my portfolio to be relatively stable. Slow but steady growth suits me, as long as I stay ahead of inflation. Income is an important secondary consideration; capital growth is not.	Low
I don't want to experience capital losses. I want my funds invested in only the most stable, secure places, and I do not wish to experience fluctuations in value greater than 5% to 10%. I am willing to experience periods when my real aftertax return (investment returns after taxes and inflation) are negative in order to achieve this safety.	Very Low

Asset Allocation Worksheet

Part 3: Suggested Portfolio Allocation

The table below suggests a sample portfolio allocation consisting of stocks, bonds, and money market funds for each risk tolerance identified in Part 2. Note that if you have significant short-term financial obligations and goals, investments in equities should be limited regardless of your risk tolerance.

| | Suggested Allocation | | |
	Stocks	Bonds	Money Market
Risk Tolerance			
Very High	90%	5%	5%
High	80%	10%	10%
Moderate	50%	30%	20%
Moderately Low	30%	50%	20%
Low	15%	50%	35%
Very Low	10%	40%	50%

Part 4: Your Portfolio Allocation—Expected Real Rate of Return

NOTE: In this section you compute the anticipated real rate of return from the suggested portfolio allocation determined in Part 3.

	Stocks	Bonds	Money Market
Aftertax Real Return (from Part 1)			
x Portfolio Allocation (from Part 3)			
Aftertax Weighted Return			
	A	B	C

Add the aftertax weighted returns identified above (A, B, and C). This is your expected real rate of return from the suggested portfolio allocation.

You may find that this return is insufficient to finance the goals you have established elsewhere in this book. If so, you should reconsider your investment restrictions (that is, consider assuming more investment risk) or else scale down your financial objectives to a more realistic level.

Investment Tracking Worksheet

Name on Account:

Type of Account:

NOTE: Use this worksheet to keep track of investments for performance measurement and tax reporting purposes.

Investments Sold This Year

Name of Security	# Units	Date Acquired	Price per Unit	Total Cost	Date Sold	Net Proceeds	Gain/ Loss	Int/Div Prior to Sale

Investments Retained

Name of Security	# Units	Date Acquired	Price per Unit	Total Cost	Market Price	Market Value	Unrealized Gain/Loss	Interest/ Dividends

Children's Net Worth Statement

Date:

Child:

	Current Value	Tax Cost (A)	Potential Tax on Sale (B)	Net Value
Bank Accounts				
Money Market Funds				
Bonds				
Stocks				
Other Assets				
Less: Loans	( )		( )	
Net Worth				

Child:

	Current Value	Tax Cost (A)	Potential Tax on Sale (B)	Net Value
Bank Accounts				
Money Market Funds				
Bonds				
Stocks				
Other Assets				
Less: Loans	( )		( )	
Net Worth				

Child:

	Current Value	Tax Cost (A)	Potential Tax on Sale (B)	Net Value
Bank Accounts				
Money Market Funds				
Bonds				
Stocks				
Other Assets				
Less: Loans	( )		( )	
Net Worth				

NOTES:

(A) Tax cost, or basis, is the amount invested in the asset for tax purposes. The greater the basis, the less the potential tax when the asset is sold.

(B) Potential tax on sale is the estimated tax due if the asset were sold immediately. Generally, investments that have been held more than one year are taxed at preferential capital gains rates.

Retirement Budget

This worksheet will help you estimate, in future dollars, the income and expenses you can expect to experience when you retire. Any shortfall (excess of expenses over income) will have to be made up from your investments. You can use the information developed here in conjunction with the Capital Sufficiency Table and the Financial Goals Worksheet (see Appendix) to determine whether your anticipated retirement portfolio is adequate to support your planned spending.

To project future amounts you will need either a financial calculator or an ordinary hand-held calculator together with a table of future values of $1. (You can use the college funding Matrix; see Appendix.) This worksheet allows you to specify a separate rate of increase for each item, since some prices (such as health care) have historically increased at rates different from the general rate of inflation.

Number of Years to Retirement:

Income	Current Year	Rate of Increase	Estimate at Retirement
Your Earnings		n/a	
Your Pension		n/a	
Domestic Partner Earnings (Opt.)		n/a	
Domestic Partner Pension (Opt.)		n/a	
Your Social Security		n/a	
Domestic Partner Social Security (Opt.)		n/a	
Other			
Other			
Total Income			

Expenses
Fixed Expenses

	Current Year	Rate of Increase	Estimate at Retirement
Taxes & Withholding			
Groceries			
Mortgage			
Other Loans & Credit Crads			
Property Tax			
Utilities			
Home Maintenance			
Clothing & Dry Cleaning			
Uninsured Medical & Dental			
Child Care			
Car Loans			
Gasoline & Oil			
Car Repairs & Maintenance			
Insurance: Life, Home, Car			
Tuition			
Total Fixed Expenses			

Variable Expenses

	Current Year	Rate of Increase	Estimate at Retirement
Major Purchases			
Restaurants			
Entertainment			
Telephone			
Vacation			
Books, CDs, Magazines			
Fitness			
Personal Grooming			
Gifts			
Charitable Donations			
Other			
Total Variable Expenses			
Total Expenses			
SURPLUS OR SHORT FALL			

Income Tax Projections

NOTE: You can use this worksheet to compute your own tax liability (Column A), your domestic partner's liability (Column B), and, if you may be eligible to file jointly (i.e., legally married on the last day of the year), your joint liability. This worksheet provides only a rough estimate, especially at higher income levels; the tax laws are complex and subject to frequent change. Consult your own tax advisor for specific guidance.

Current values for tax rates, standard deductions, personal exemptions, and other amounts can be found in IRS Publication 17 or the instructions to Form 1040.

	Column A — You	Column B — Your Domestic Partner	Column C — Filing Jointly
Gross Income			
Taxable Wages/Salaries			
Taxable Dividends and Interest			
Net Business Income (Loss)			
Net Capital Gain (Loss)			
Net Rent Income (Loss)			
Net Partnership Income (Loss)			
Other Income (Loss)			
Total Gross Income			
Adjustments to Gross Income			
Alimony Paid			
IRA Payments			
Keogh Plan Payments			
Other Adjustments			
Total Adjustments to Gross Income			
Adjusted Gross Income			
Itemized Deductions			
Medical			
Taxes			
Mortgage Interest Paid			
Other Interest Paid			
Charitable Contributions			
Casualty and Theft Losses			
Unreimbursed Moving Expenses			
Unreimbursed Employee Business Deductions			
Miscellaneous Deductions			
Reduction for Income Limitations	( )	( )	( )
Total Itemized Deductions			
Standard Deduction			
Greater of Itemized Deductions or Standard Deduction			
Allowable Exemptions (number)			
Allowable Exemptions ($ value)			
Total Deductions and Exemptions			
Taxable Income (AGI - Deductions & Exemptions)			
TAX (If you have capital gains, see instructions for Form 1040, Schedule D; otherwise use applicable tables or tax rate schedules.			

Estate-Tax Projection

Part 1: Compute Your Gross Estate

In this section you will compute the *gross estate*, which is the amount of property potentially subject to federal estate tax upon your death. Include all property owned by you and, if you are not married, all jointly owned property, unless your survivors can show you contributed only a certain percentage of the original cost. For example, assume you are joint owner of a piece of land worth $100,000 and the other owner is your domestic partner. If you cannot prove how much you contributed to the cost, include the entire $100,000 in your gross estate (even if you contributed nothing). However, if you can prove that you contributed only part of the cost, include only the portion of the value that reflects the percentage you contributed.

Gross Estate	Current Value
Liquid Assets	
Less: Life Insurance Cash Value	( )
Investment Assets	
Personal Assets	
Total Assets	
Short-Term Debt	
Long-Term Debt	
Total Debt	
Net Worth (Total Assets - Total Debt)	
Net Worth (computed above)	
Insurance on Your Life Owned by You	
Gift Taxes Paid in Last 3 Years	
Property Subject to "Claw-Back" Rules Within Past 3 Years	
Gross Estate	

Part 2: Compute Your Estate Tax

Gross Estate	
Less: Estimated Funeral Expenses	( )
Estate Administration	( )
Adjusted Gross Estate	
Less: Marital Deduction	( )
Charitable Deduction	( )
Taxable Estate	
Add: Adjusted Taxable Gifts	
Tentative Tax Base	
Tentative Estate Tax (from table on pages 152–53)	
Less: Unified Credit	($192,800)
Gift Taxes Paid on Lifetime Gifts	( )
State Death Tax Credit	( )
Other Credits	( )
Net Estate Tax	

Insurance Summary

Name:

Part 4: Homeowner's

	Policy 1	Policy 2	Policy 3
Insurance Company			
Policy Number			
Insured Property			
Annual Premium			
Policy Type	HO-	HO-	HO-
Policy Limit—Dwelling			
Policy Limit—Contents			
Policy Limit—Liability			
Automatic Inflation Adjustment			
Cost to Replace Dwelling			
Market Value of Dwelling (except land)			
Replacement Cost Coverage			
Deductible			
Required Co-Insurance Percentage			

Part 5: Automobile

	Policy 1	Policy 2	Policy 3
Insurance Company			
Policy Number			
Insured Vehicle			
Annual Premium			
Principal Driver	HO-	HO-	HO-
Other Drivers			
Liability Limits—Bodily Injury (per person)			
Liability Limits—Bodily Injury (per accident)			
Liability Limits—Property Damage			
Collision Coverage? (if yes, deductible)			
Comprehensive Coverage?(if yes, deductible)			
Medical Payments			
Uninsured Motorist Coverage			

College Funding Matrix

NOTE: This table shows the effect of inflation on $1,000 of today's college costs. For example, a college that costs $10,000 per year today would cost $14,800 in 10 years if costs rise by 4% per year.

INFLATION RATE	Year									
	1	2	3	4	5	6	7	8	9	10
1%	$1,010	$1,020	$1,030	$1,041	$1,051	$1,062	$1,072	$1,083	$1,094	$1,105
2%	$1,020	$1,040	$1,061	$1,082	$1,104	$1,126	$1,149	$1,172	$1,195	$1,219
3%	$1,030	$1,061	$1,093	$1,126	$1,159	$1,194	$1,230	$1,267	$1,305	$1,344
4%	$1,040	$1,082	$1,125	$1,170	$1,217	$1,265	$1,316	$1,369	$1,423	$1,480
5%	$1,050	$1,103	$1,158	$1,216	$1,276	$1,340	$1,407	$1,477	$1,551	$1,629
6%	$1,060	$1,124	$1,191	$1,262	$1,338	$1,419	$1,504	$1,594	$1,689	$1,791
7%	$1,070	$1,145	$1,225	$1,311	$1,403	$1,501	$1,606	$1,718	$1,838	$1,967
8%	$1,080	$1,166	$1,260	$1,360	$1,469	$1,587	$1,714	$1,851	$1,999	$2,159
9%	$1,090	$1,188	$1,295	$1,412	$1,539	$1,677	$1,828	$1,993	$2,172	$2,367
10%	$1,100	$1,210	$1,331	$1,464	$1,611	$1,772	$1,949	$2,144	$2,358	$2,594
11%	$1,110	$1,232	$1,368	$1,518	$1,685	$1,870	$2,076	$2,305	$2,558	$2,839
12%	$1,120	$1,254	$1,405	$1,574	$1,762	$1,974	$2,211	$2,476	$2,773	$3,106

INFLATION RATE	Year									
	11	12	13	14	15	16	17	18	19	20
1%	$1,116	$1,127	$1,138	$1,149	$1,161	$1,173	$1,184	$1,196	$1,208	$1,220
2%	$1,243	$1,268	$1,294	$1,319	$1,346	$1,373	$1,400	$1,428	$1,457	$1,486
3%	$1,384	$1,426	$1,469	$1,513	$1,558	$1,605	$1,653	$1,702	$1,754	$1,806
4%	$1,539	$1,601	$1,665	$1,732	$1,801	$1,873	$1,948	$2,026	$2,107	$2,191
5%	$1,710	$1,796	$1,886	$1,980	$2,079	$2,183	$2,292	$2,407	$2,527	$2,653
6%	$1,898	$2,012	$2,133	$2,261	$2,397	$2,540	$2,693	$2,854	$3,026	$3,207
7%	$2,105	$2,252	$2,410	$2,579	$2,759	$2,952	$3,159	$3,380	$3,617	$3,870
8%	$2,332	$2,518	$2,720	$2,937	$3,172	$3,426	$3,700	$3,996	$4,316	$4,661
9%	$2,580	$2,813	$3,066	$3,342	$3,642	$3,970	$4,328	$4,717	$5,142	$5,604
10%	$2,853	$3,138	$3,452	$3,797	$4,177	$4,595	$5,054	$5,560	$6,116	$6,727
11%	$3,152	$3,498	$3,883	$4,310	$4,785	$5,311	$5,895	$6,544	$7,263	$8,062
12%	$3,479	$3,896	$4,363	$4,887	$5,474	$6,130	$6,866	$7,690	$8,613	$9,646

INFLATION RATE	Year									
	21	22	23	24	25	26	27	28	29	30
1%	$1,232	$1,245	$1,257	$1,270	$1,282	$1,295	$1,308	$1,321	$1,335	$1,348
2%	$1,516	$1,546	$1,577	$1,608	$1,641	$1,673	$1,707	$1,741	$1,776	$1,811
3%	$1,860	$1,916	$1,974	$2,033	$2,094	$2,157	$2,221	$2,288	$2,357	$2,427
4%	$2,279	$2,370	$2,465	$2,563	$2,666	$2,772	$2,883	$2,999	$3,119	$3,243
5%	$2,786	$2,925	$3,072	$3,225	$3,386	$3,556	$3,733	$3,920	$4,116	$4,322
6%	$3,400	$3,604	$3,820	$4,049	$4,292	$4,549	$4,822	$5,112	$5,418	$5,743
7%	$4,141	$4,430	$4,741	$5,072	$5,427	$5,807	$6,214	$6,649	$7,114	$7,612
8%	$5,034	$5,437	$5,871	$6,341	$6,848	$7,396	$7,988	$8,627	$9,317	$10,063
9%	$6,109	$6,659	$7,258	$7,911	$8,623	$9,399	$10,245	$11,167	$12,172	$13,268
10%	$7,400	$8,140	$8,954	$9,850	$10,835	$11,918	$13,110	$14,421	$15,863	$17,449
11%	$8,949	$9,934	$11,026	$12,239	$13,585	$15,080	$16,739	$18,580	$20,624	$22,892
12%	$10,804	$12,100	$13,552	$15,179	$17,000	$19,040	$21,325	$23,884	$26,750	$29,960

Inflation Matrix

NOTE: This table shows the effect of inflation on $1,000 of today's purchasing power. For example, $1,000 today will be worth $614 in purchasing power after 10 years at 5% inflation.

INFLATION RATE	Year 1	2	3	4	5	6	7	8	9	10
1%	$990	$980	$971	$961	$951	$942	$933	$923	$914	$905
2%	$980	$961	$942	$924	$906	$888	$871	$853	$837	$820
3%	$971	$943	$915	$888	$863	$837	$813	$789	$766	$744
4%	$962	$925	$889	$855	$822	$790	$760	$731	$703	$676
5%	$952	$907	$864	$823	$784	$746	$711	$677	$645	$614
6%	$943	$890	$840	$792	$747	$705	$665	$627	$592	$558
7%	$935	$873	$816	$763	$713	$666	$623	$582	$544	$508
8%	$926	$857	$794	$735	$681	$630	$583	$540	$500	$463
9%	$917	$842	$772	$708	$650	$596	$547	$502	$460	$422
10%	$909	$826	$751	$683	$621	$564	$513	$467	$424	$386
11%	$901	$812	$731	$659	$593	$535	$482	$434	$391	$352
12%	$893	$797	$712	$636	$567	$507	$452	$404	$361	$322

INFLATION RATE	Year 11	12	13	14	15	16	17	18	19	20
1%	$896	$887	$879	$870	$861	$853	$844	$836	$828	$820
2%	$804	$788	$773	$758	$743	$728	$714	$700	$686	$673
3%	$722	$701	$681	$661	$642	$623	$605	$587	$570	$554
4%	$650	$625	$601	$577	$555	$534	$513	$494	$475	$456
5%	$585	$557	$530	$505	$481	$458	$436	$416	$396	$377
6%	$527	$497	$469	$442	$417	$394	$371	$350	$331	$312
7%	$475	$444	$415	$388	$362	$339	$317	$296	$277	$258
8%	$429	$397	$368	$340	$315	$292	$270	$250	$232	$215
9%	$388	$356	$326	$299	$275	$252	$231	$212	$194	$178
10%	$350	$319	$290	$263	$239	$218	$198	$180	$164	$149
11%	$317	$286	$258	$232	$209	$188	$170	$153	$138	$124
12%	$287	$257	$229	$205	$183	$163	$146	$130	$116	$104

INFLATION RATE	Year 21	22	23	24	25	26	27	28	29	30
1%	$811	$803	$795	$788	$780	$772	$764	$757	$749	$742
2%	$660	$647	$634	$622	$610	$598	$586	$574	$563	$552
3%	$538	$522	$507	$492	$478	$464	$450	$437	$424	$412
4%	$439	$422	$406	$390	$375	$361	$347	$333	$321	$308
5%	$359	$342	$326	$310	$295	$281	$268	$255	$243	$231
6%	$294	$278	$262	$247	$233	$220	$207	$196	$185	$174
7%	$242	$226	$211	$197	$184	$172	$161	$150	$141	$131
8%	$199	$184	$170	$158	$146	$135	$125	$116	$107	$99
9%	$164	$150	$138	$126	$116	$106	$98	$90	$82	$75
10%	$135	$123	$112	$102	$92	$84	$76	$69	$63	$57
11%	$112	$101	$91	$82	$74	$66	$60	$54	$48	$44
12%	$93	$83	$74	$66	$59	$53	$47	$42	$37	$33

Capital Sufficiency Table

NOTE: This table helps you estimate how long your retirement nest egg will last, regardless of inflation. You must estimate the real (after taxes and inflation) rate of return on your investments, and also the level of withdrawals (in today's dollars) that you wish to maintain during retirement. Then, find the "capital-to- expense ratio" by dividing your estimated withdrawals into your nest egg. (For example, if your retirement fund is $200,000 and your estimated withdrawal level is $20,000, your capital-to-expense ratio is 10.) Find the box that corresponds to your expected return and your capital-to-expense ratio, and you will know how many years you will be able to afford your projected withdrawals.

Capital-to-Expense Ratio	INVESTMENT YIELD (AFTER TAXES AND INFLATION)							
	-2%	-1%	0%	1%	2%	3%	4%	5%
100	55	69	100	*	*	*	*	*
90	51	64	90	*	*	*	*	*
80	47	58	80	*	*	*	*	*
70	43	53	70	*	*	*	*	*
60	39	47	60	90	*	*	*	*
50	34	40	50	68	*	*	*	*
40	29	33	40	50	77	*	*	*
30	23	26	30	35	44	70	*	*
25	20	22	25	28	34	44	83	*
20	16	18	20	22	25	29	37	62
19	16	17	19	20	23	27	33	48
18	15	16	18	19	21	25	30	39
17	14	15	17	18	20	23	27	33
16	13	14	16	17	19	21	24	29
15	13	14	15	16	17	19	21	25
14	12	13	14	14	16	17	19	22
13	11	12	13	13	14	16	17	19
12	10	11	12	12	13	14	15	17
11	10	10	11	11	12	13	14	15
10	9	9	10	10	11	11	12	13
9	8	8	9	9	9	10	10	11
8	7	7	8	8	8	8	9	9
7	6	6	7	7	7	7	7	8
6	5	5	6	6	6	6	6	6
5	4	4	5	5	5	5	5	5
4	2	3	4	4	4	4	4	4
3	2	2	3	3	3	3	3	3
	YEARS UNTIL CAPITAL IS EXHAUSTED							

Index